IS TINY DANCER REALLY ELTON'S LITTLE JOHN?

IS TINY DANCER REALLY ELTON'S LITTLE JOHN?

MUSIC'S MOST ENDURING MYSTERIES, MYTHS, AND RUMORS REVEALED

GAVIN EDWARDS

THREE RIVERS PRESS · NEW YORK

Published in the United States by Three Rivers Press, an imprint of the
Crown Publishing Group, a division of Random House, Inc., New York.
www.crownpublishing.com

Three Rivers Press and the Tugboat design are registered trademarks of
Random House, Inc.

Portions of this book were previously published, sometimes in different
form, in *Rolling Stone*.

Library of Congress Cataloging-in-Publication Data
Edwards, Gavin, 1968–
    Is tiny dancer really Elton's little John? : music's most enduring
mysteries, myths, and rumors revealed / Gavin Edwards. — 1st ed.
            p. cm.
    Includes bibliographical references.
    1. Rock music—Anecdotes. 2. Rock musicians—Anecdotes. I.Title.
    ML3534.E3 2006
    781.66—dc22
2006012161

ISBN-13: 978-0-307-34603-2
ISBN-10: 0-307-34603-X

Printed in the United States of America

Design by Kay Schuckhart / Blond on Pond

10 9 8 7 6 5 4 3 2

First Edition

For Jen, the best dance partner ever

IS TINY DANCER REALLY ELTON'S LITTLE JOHN?

Rock songs, you may have noticed, are full of questions. How many roads must a man walk down before you can call him a man? Do you know the way to San Jose? Can your pussy do the dog? Is it hard to make arrangements with yourself when you're old enough to repay but young enough to sell? Scaramouche, Scaramouche, can you do the fandango?

The best music makes you want to answer all those questions. (For example: five; not without Google Maps; with enough lubricant; yes; let me get my fandango shoes on.) That's not where the questions end, of course. Rock music (and by "rock," I mean "the whole megillah of popular music since 1955, based on the union of blues and country, but encompassing soul, folk, hip-hop, distorted electric guitars, and the funky chicken") inspires entire new lines of inquiries. If you've ever wasted hours ingesting intravenous MTV, or spent an afternoon with headphones on, trying to decipher the lyrics of either 50 Cent or Michael Stipe, you know the landscape of modern music is a strange place, weirder than even its most devout fans sometimes realize.

That doesn't stop them from going on a quest for knowledge, not unlike the one for fire engaged in by Rae Dawn Chong. Once you start asking questions, you never stop. Why is Metallica's "One" in waltz time? Why didn't the word *hateration* from Mary J. Blige's "Family Affair" catch on? If you stripped Tom Petty and Bob Seger to the waist and gave them each a machete, who would win in a fight?

For several years, I wrote a column in *Rolling Stone* called "*Rolling Stone* Knows," where I answered similarly inscrutable queries from the magazine's readers. I avoided trivia stumpers designed to test the boundaries of my knowledge—they just weren't that interesting. ("The guitarist for Strawberry Alarm Clock went on to play in what band?" asked one letter; the answer is, of course, Lynyrd Skynyrd.) If you want to use any of the contents of this book in trivia contests, well, who could blame you? But my goal was to increase the human race's sum total of rock knowledge, one question at a time. That meant debunking or detailing myths, researching the half-forgotten origins of favorite songs, and uncovering the secrets of music in general.

So, if you want to know what grades Mick Jagger got while he was a student at the London School of Economics, turn to page 203. If you yearn to know the secret meaning behind the Guns N' Roses album title *"The Spaghetti Incident?"* you should head to page 49. And if you'd like to know the answer to the question that this book's title poses—in "Tiny Dancer," is Elton John actually singing to his penis?—then I suggest you head to page 126. Or you could keep reading this introduction; it'll be over soon enough, anyway, and then the questions start.

This book not only compiles material from my column, it expands many of the answers (there wasn't always space in the magazine to give as detailed a response as I would have liked) and adds dozens of new entries. For the most part, however, I stayed away from questions of judgment. If you want to know the five greatest rappers in history, the ten best Bob Dylan songs, or the three greatest uses of the woodblock, you've come to the wrong place. It's not that I'm shy with my opinions, as anyone who's ever had dinner with me will attest. In my life, I've written literally hundreds of record reviews; musical opinions bubble out of me like natural spring water from, well, a natural spring.

But when you look up something in this volume, I want you to be rest assured that it's as thoroughly researched and documented as possible; if an answer is a matter of conjecture or my opinion, it's clearly labeled as such.

Rock music also asks questions without words, interrogations that express the primal longings of the human heart. A rough translation of the best possible answer to most of those questions: Yes, I do want to get up and dance with you.

1 MYSTERY ACHIEVEMENT

Exploring the Strange Byways of Rock

Of all the bands I've ever met, the one most fully committed to the absurdity of rock 'n' roll was probably the Darkness. And considering that I once interviewed Spinal Tap's David St. Hubbins (Michael McKean, staying in character on the phone), that's no small praise. But the Darkness bring a lot to the party: catsuits, an insane falsetto, and a video where a pterodactyl humps a spaceship.

This was the philosophy of lead singer Justin Hawkins: "Less is more? That's bollocks. *More* is more. That's why it's called 'more.' If it was actually less, it'd be called 'less.' "

There's something about rock 'n' roll that brings out the smoke machines, secret backward messages, and other strange experiments. Hawkins, unsurprisingly, has a philosophy about such matters. He told me, "My favorite catchphrase is 'If something's worth doing, it's worth overdoing.' Even subtlety. If you're going to be subtle, you should *really fucking be subtle.*"

● ● ●

I heard that Stevie Wonder lost his sense of smell. Is that true?

Yes—but he got better. Blind since infancy, Wonder was in a serious car accident on August 6, 1973, while on tour in North Carolina. (No, he wasn't driving.) His cousin John Harris was chauffeuring him from Greenville to Durham on Interstate 85, heading for a concert to benefit a black radio station. Wonder had his headphones on and was listening to the two-track mix of *Innervisions.* When the logging truck they were following hit its brakes, Harris tried to swerve around it but didn't quite succeed. A log from the truck smashed through the windshield and hit Wonder in the face. Wonder was in a coma for four days; his associates knew he was feeling better only when he started grabbing at nurses. Only twenty-three years old at the time of the accident, Wonder had lost his sense of smell and gained a scar on his forehead. He simultaneously lost his sense of taste—which some would say explains the existence of "I Just Called to Say I Love You." Fortunately, Wonder largely recovered. "I lost my sense of smell a little bit, my sense of taste for a minute," he said. "But I'm pretty straight. I came out at the end of it with the blessing of life."

Lenny Kravitz thinks Stevie Wonder's one of the two greatest drummers ever: see p. 202 in Chapter 15.

• • •

What's an MBE, anyway? Why did John Lennon give his back?

The MBE (Member of the Order of the British Empire) was an award invented by King George V in 1917 to commemorate services to the war effort by people who weren't at the frontlines. All the Beatles received the medal in 1965, which entitled them to a payment of forty pounds a year and free admission to the Whispering Gallery at St. Paul's Cathedral (ordinarily about a shilling). The Beatles were somewhat mystified as to why the Queen

was honoring them, but they were generally
cheerful about the notion. As Ringo Starr put it,
"We're going to meet the Queen and she's going
to give us a badge. I thought, 'This is cool.' "
Lennon later said that the Beatles had gotten
stoned at Buckingham Palace before the cere-
mony, smoking a joint in the bathroom; George
Harrison said it was just tobacco. When the
Beatles finally met Queen Elizabeth II, they
thought that her majesty was a pretty nice girl,
but she didn't have a lot to say. (Really.)

The Beatles' parents were pleased by the
awards. The group members themselves largely
forgot about their medals, although Harrison and
Paul McCartney later used theirs as jacket
decorations at the *Sgt. Pepper's Lonely Hearts
Club Band* photo shoot. Lennon, meanwhile, gave
his to his beloved Aunt Mimi, who hung it over
her mantelpiece. But as the years went by, he had
second thoughts about his implied endorsement
of the British government and the royal family, so
on November 25, 1969, he sent the medal back to
the Queen, seizing on whatever excuse seemed
handy. His accompanying note read, "Your
Majesty, I am returning this MBE in protest
against Britain's involvement in the Nigeria-Biafra
thing, against our support of America in Vietnam
and against 'Cold Turkey' slipping down the

charts. With love, John Lennon." (When the region of Biafra attempted to break away from Nigeria in the late '60s and a civil war ensued, Great Britain provided the ruling party with air support. Lennon's solo single "Cold Turkey" peaked on the U.K. charts at number fourteen.) Lennon said at the time,

In 1965, the Beatles also checked out LSD—which they got from a dentist. What the hell was a dentist doing turning them on? See p. 154 in Chapter 11.

"The Queen's intelligent. It won't spoil her cornflakes."

● ● ●

Why does Dave Grohl of the Foo Fighters chew gum when he sings and plays live? Is there a reason for this, or is it just a bad habit?

"It's just to keep my throat and mouth lubricated," Grohl has said. He's decided that masticating a wad of gum lets him scream better: "I don't choke and vomit." Grohl, who favors Dentyne Ice, has joked, "Onstage I need a mintyfresh microphone." Chewing gum is an easier way of achieving that winter-fresh aroma than dipping all the Foo Fighters' equipment in Listerine, of course, but sometimes his gum habit results in technical complications. At a live performance in 1997, Grohl got his sugary saliva all over the microphone, attracting the attention of a bee; for the rest of the show, whenever Grohl tried to sing, the bee would chase after him.

For details of a different onstage mishap, check out what happened when Iggy Pop shaved off his eyebrows on p. 176 of Chapter 13.

• • •

What was the flip side to the original "Rock Around the Clock" by Bill Haley and the Comets?

Although people can and do argue for hours about what the very first rock single was, "Rock Around the Clock" was unquestionably the first rock single to hit number one, in the summer of 1955. Its blockbuster success was sparked by its use on the soundtrack of the movie *The Blackboard Jungle.* But the year before, the 78-rpm single of "Rock Around the Clock" had been a flop—and it was only a B-side itself. The song that took top billing over it was "Thirteen Women," a novelty R&B number about an H-bomb explosion that leaves just fourteen people alive: one man and thirteen women. Lyrics such as "I had three girls dancing the mambo / Three girls balling the jack" were apparently one year ahead of their time.

● ● ●

In the movie *Moulin Rouge*, Kylie Minogue is credited as "The Green Fairy," but Ozzy Osbourne is credited as "Voice of the Green Fairy." Can you clear this up?

In the movie, after Ewan McGregor drinks absinthe for the first time, he has a vision of a small emerald sprite, who announces, "I'm the Green Fairy!" She flies about, sprinkling pixie dust and warbling, "The hills are alive with the sound of music." The fairy is clearly played by Kylie Minogue—and sounds like her, too. If these vocals came from Ozzy, he must've been sucking down helium before the Foley session. At the very end of the hallucination, however, Kylie's eyes turn red and she screams—and that scream sounds like the Prince of Fuckin' Darkness. "I feel that Kylie's contribution to the film is certainly undercredited," *Moulin Rouge* director Baz Luhrmann told me via email. "The high, clear 'Sound of Music' in a quasi-operatic style is Kylie—who, I have to say, has more vocal dexterity than people could imagine. The scream at the very end is in fact

Ozzy Osbourne. The story behind this is that at one stage I had a much more complicated sequence where the innocent Green Fairy metamorphoses into its darker demonic alter ego. With the ever-helpful Sharon Osbourne, we recorded Ozzy doing 'The Sound of Music' for that sequence—but we ended up cutting down his incredible vocal to a brief scream."

• • •

What are all those initials in the Sex Pistols' "Anarchy in the U.K."? MPLA? UDA?

It's an alphabet soup of civil-war references from '70s headlines: either a suggestion of what could happen in the U.K. itself (that's the United Kingdom, of course) or a lyrical holiday in other people's misery. The IRA and the UDA were the largest paramilitary armies in the conflict in Northern Ireland; the heavily armed IRA (Irish Republican Army) were on the Republican (anti-British, pro-unification) side, while the thousands-strong UDA (Ulster Defence Association) were on the Loyalist (pro-British, anti-unification) side. The MPLA were farther away: They're the political group that took control of Angola, formerly one of Portugal's African colonies, in the 1975–76 civil war there, and they still run the country today. (The initials stand for Movimento Popular de Libertação de Angola, or the Popular Movement for the Liberation of Angola.) Be grateful that Johnny Rotten didn't rattle off the competing Angolan factions, the FNLA and the UNITA. One other acronym you may have missed: When Rotten sings, "I use the enemy," it's a deliberate homonym for "I use the NME," or *New Musical Express,* the British weekly music newspaper. No civil war there, unless you count their rivalry with *Melody Maker.*

> Johnny Rotten wasn't the first candidate for Sex Pistols lead singer; see p. 75 of Chapter 6.

Johnny Rotten wasn't the first candidate for Sex Pistols lead singer; see p. 75 of Chapter 6.

● ● ●

Who is the dude with the umbrella in OutKast's video for "The Way You Move"? I think I am in love with him.

He's Farnsworth (also "Fonzworth") Bentley, arguably the most dapper man in hip-hop. "It's a tradition in my family that when a gentleman turns twenty-five, he gets a fedora," he told me. "In another twenty years, my generation's going to be passing down velour jogging suits—that's not stylish." He added, "If you don't know how to tie a bow tie, that's like not being able to drive a stick." In addition to the OutKast video, Bentley has appeared in videos for Usher and P. Diddy, and in the movie *Honey*. He was also featured in MTV's *Making the Band 2*. "Half the things you see me in, I sneak into," he said.

Bentley is the alter ego of the extremely sharp Derek Watkins, who grew up in Atlanta with André Benjamin (aka Andre 3000 of OutKast) and graduated from Morehouse College in 1997. When he moved to New York, he became known on the hip-hop scene for being impeccably dressed; in 2001, P. Diddy hired him as his assistant and dubbed him "Farnsworth." Watkins said, "I set out to create buzz for my brand. I wanted to turn myself into a character like Fire Marshall Bill or Mork from Ork." It paid off when he was photographed holding an umbrella over P. Diddy in St. Tropez, and was identified as Diddy's butler. "It was all a big hustle," he confided.

Watkins is currently working on various media projects and developing his own line of umbrellas. "I eventually will hire an agent and a publicist," he said, "but I want to see how much I can hustle for myself."

● ● ●

What does that guy say at the end of Radiohead's video for "Just"?

In case you've never seen the video—from Radiohead's excellent second album, *The Bends*—it's got two components. One is the band, looking misanthropic and unwashed, giving it their all as they pantomime rocking out in an apartment. The other is a narrative, filmed in a style reminiscent of director Douglas Sirk: A well-dressed man, an archetypal businessman, suddenly lies down in the middle of the sidewalk, curled up as if he wants his blanket. Someone trips over him, and then discovers that the man doesn't want to get up. He says he's not drunk or crazy, but despite the entreaties of a gathering crowd, he won't get up and won't explain why he's on the pavement, although he denies that it's cheap nihilism or fear of death. (This dialogue is all communicated through subtitles; Radiohead provides the subtext with the song's chorus of "you do it to yourself.") Finally, he tells the crowd why he's lying down, at which point the subtitles are abandoned and the editing becomes choppy enough to prevent effective lip-reading. The band members gaze down from a window as the people below all lie down.

In case you haven't figured it out by now, the

whole point of the video is not what the man says, which is meant to be as much of a mystery as whatever it is Bill Murray whispers into Scarlett Johansson's ear at the end of *Lost in Translation.* The band remains resolutely silent on the issue; Jamie Thraves, the director of the clip, has said, "To tell you would deaden the impact, and probably make you want to lie down in the road, too." You want a real mystery? Why does the crowd on a British street include an American police officer?

For the word on Radiohead's *Kid A,* turn to p. 46 of Chapter 3.

● ● ●

A friend of mine said he heard that Tom Waits has a tattoo on his chest of a restaurant's menu. Is this true?

Tom Waits has never let the facts get in the way of a good story. He has plenty of tattoos, but none of them includes the soup du jour. Waits spent his youth in National City, a suburb of San Diego, where he worked at Napoleone's Pizza House. As he told the tale, "I got a map of Easter Island on my back.

Tom Waits spent years in a relationship with Rickie Lee Jones; get some of the details on p. 138 of Chapter 10.

And I have the full menu from Napoleone's Pizza House on my stomach. After a while, they dispensed with the menus: They'd send me out, and I'd take my shirt off and stand by the tables."

• • •

S_O how tall is Bono, anyway?

Not very. For decades, the only official word on this matter was a questionnaire filled out by somebody at the U2 World Service, where Bono was listed as five-foot-eight. Let's just say that measurement was optimistic, presumably based on the theory that if Bono kept drinking his milk, he'd grow up real tall one day. According to the online U2 FAQ, Bono's pal Gavin Friday has recently given Bono's height as five-foot-six-and-a-half.

So how do we double-check that height? In New York City, where I live, it's not hard to find women who have literally bumped into Bono at an airport, stood next to him at a party, or passed by him on the sidewalk outside the restaurant Balthazar, to pick just three female friends of mine. (And he macked on only some of them: The friend outside Balthazar got treated to a long, up-and-down leer. "He was like a construction worker," reports an eyewitness, "only with

> Stretching to grow tall, running to stand still: The last word on a U2 song-writing trick can be found on p. 137 of Chapter 10.

expensive eyewear.") At any rate, gauging against their own heights, and taking into consideration the fact that Bono was sometimes wearing visible heels, all three agreed that Bono seemed to be five-foot-six.

• • •

A friend told me that while the Clash were still recording, Joe Strummer ran a marathon in a chicken suit—can this be true?

The late, great Strummer ran in *three* marathons while the Clash were active, none of them in a chicken suit, alas. In 1981, after the release of *Sandinista!,* he completed the London Marathon with no training whatsoever, confirming his status as one of the stubbornest men in rock. In 1982, just as *Combat Rock* was coming out, Strummer disappeared for almost a month, either as a publicity stunt or as a power play. (Drummer Topper Headon has said that Strummer wanted to fire him, but first needed to demonstrate his own indispensability to the band.) Strummer had decamped to Paris, where he ran in another

marathon. The following
year, he ran the London
Marathon *again,* complet-
ing the route in four
hours and thirty minutes

The ultimate
outcome of the Clash's
power plays is on
p. 78 of Chapter 6.

and resisting the temptation to duck into
a pub along the way.

● ● ●

Somebody said there's a secret
map on Weezer's *Pinkerton,* but I can't find it.
Help!

What's at the center of your *Pinkerton* disc? If you
say "a hole," you're ready for the next step: Place
your disc in its jewel-box tray and look through
that hole, peeping like a voyeur into the obses-
sions of Rivers Cuomo. You will see something
that looks like a little piece of a map. And now, if
you pry out the entire tray, you will find what
looks like a vintage map of Japan, labeled ISOLA
DELLA FARFALLA.

On the surface, this just reinforces the album's
theme—the opera *Madame Butterfly.* "I would
listen to nothing but opera, given the choice,"
Cuomo told me in 1996. "I saw *Madame Butterfly*
in L.A., and my face was caked with snot and

tears and my chest was heaving. *Pinkerton* is named after a character in that opera." In Puccini's opera, Pinkerton is the British army cad who goes to Japan, marries the geisha Cio-Cio San, and then abandons her, driving her to suicide. Any resemblance to Cuomo's own fickle ways is purely intentional.

If you look more closely at the map, however, you will begin to notice a host of anachronistic details, starting with the Weezer "W" logo placed over the legend. Various geographical points have been renamed—some for *Butterfly* characters, others for people important to Cuomo, including Joe Matt (creator of the confessional comic *Peepshow*), Camille Paglia (academic gender provocateur), and Mykel and Carli (presidents of the Weezer fan club, also commemorated in the Weezer B-side "Mykel and Carli," recently reissued on the deluxe edition of the Blue Album). The whole effort is credited to "Republica di Yngwie," a reference to the polar opposite of Puccini: guitar shredder Yngwie Malmsteen.

The tale of how Weezer got their name (and some of Cuomo's other band monikers) awaits on p. 182 of Chapter 13.

● ● ●

I heard that John Mayer actually sees music as colors—does that just mean he gets stoned a lot?

No, he has an unusual neurological condition called synaesthesia. People with synaesthesia overlay sensory perceptions in an unusual fashion: They might perceive the letter Q as orange, for instance, or the number five as minty. This isn't just a flight of fancy; for synaesthetes, these perceptions are fundamental and unchanging, the way you might unfailingly describe the number eight as "curvy." Mayer's variety of synaesthesia means that when he hears music, he associates colors with it. (Although synaesthesia is relatively rare—by some estimates, just 1 in 25,000 people has it—other musicians who may have had the condition in some degree include composer Franz Liszt and guitarist Jimi Hendrix.)

So how does Mayer hear some of his own songs? I called him to ask. "No Such Thing": "Red over white." "Your Body Is a Wonderland": "White, or clear. Diamond." "83": "Yellow and red and avocado." Is the music he loves usually in one part of the color spectrum? "I go for rainbow stuff," Mayer told me. "Dave Matthews's *Under the Table and Dreaming* was like a kid breaking into a paint store. Rock music is brown and gray. I'm not a rocker. Melody is color."

● ● ●

What is that guy saying at the end of "Strawberry Fields Forever"? It sounds like "I'm very . . ." and then you can't pick up the rest of it.

"Cranberry sauce." "That guy" is John Lennon.

● ● ●

How did the "Paul Is Dead" rumor start? What were the major clues?

Well, not being able to understand "cranberry sauce" was one of them; a lot of people thought the pronouncement was "I bury Paul."

Be warned: This is like the JFK assassination (except for its not being, you know, a real death). You get interested, you read the Warren Report, and before you know it, you're up at three A.M. looking for other conspiracy theorists on the Web. But the extremely abridged version is this: The "Paul Is Dead" rumor began floating around midwestern America in 1969 (the same year the Beatles recorded *Abbey Road* and broke up). In September, the student newspaper of Drake University in Des Moines, Iowa, printed an article about the rumor, which doesn't seem to have gotten much attention. In October, however, a listener called up Detroit DJ Russ Gibb, told him McCartney was dead, laid out some of the clues, and finished by getting him to play "Revolution 9" backward. (The repeated phrase "number nine" sounded like "Turn me on, dead man.")

Subsequently, practically everything on any Beatles record became a clue in a composite narrative, which posited that McCartney had blown his mind out in a car around 1966 and been replaced by a look-alike. A few of the landmark clues: On the inside of the *Sgt. Pepper's* cover, McCartney sported an armband emblazoned with "OPD," which allegedly stood for "Officially Pronounced Dead." (Others say it's "OPP," which, as Naughty by Nature taught us all, means "Other People's Property," and some other, lewder definitions.) On the cover of the American album *Yesterday . . . and Today,* the other Beatles surround McCartney, who is sitting in a steamer trunk. But if you turn the cover counterclockwise, he appears to be in a coffin. And on the cover of *Abbey Road,* McCartney is barefoot and out of step with the other Beatles. Parked on the street behind the band is a Volkswagen Beetle with the license plate LMW 281F. "LMW" might mean any number of things, including "Linda McCartney

Weeps," but the lower half was widely inter-preted to mean "28 IF"—that is, Paul would have been twenty-eight, if only he had survived.

As with any elaborate conspiracy theory, you shouldn't expect consistency; for example, McCartney was only twenty-seven when *Abbey Road* was released. But "Paul Is Dead" stands as a charmingly loopy testament to the levels of obsession the Beatles inspired. And what did McCartney think of the greatly exaggerated reports of his death? He said, "Someone from the office rang me up and said, 'Look, Paul, you're dead.' And I said, 'Oh, I don't agree with that.' " McCartney decided it wasn't worth refuting the story right away: "It'll probably be the best publicity we've ever had, and I won't have to do a thing except stay alive."

James Taylor, who was the first outside artist signed to the Beatles' Apple label, did write a coded song about death, his classic "Fire and Rain." See p. 188 in Chapter 14 for details.

GET UR FREAK ON

Sex Lives of the Stars

Here's the logistical problem with having an active sex life on tour: Generally speaking, the band's bus rolls out of town around midnight, an hour or so after the show's over. (To save on hotel bills, most rock groups just sleep in their bunks while the bus rolls down the highway to the next city.) So if you're looking to score with a lithesome young local, you either have to work extremely quickly or convince her that although she's parked her car in Detroit, she really wants to wake up in Milwaukee.

I once witnessed Rivers Cuomo of Weezer throw caution to the wind in the pursuit of post-show nookie (this was on the *Pinkerton* tour, long before he even contemplated a vow of celibacy). We sat in a club's basement dressing room, chatting idly about drugs (his management wouldn't give him any), and then his head snapped up. "Fuck!" he shouted. "I'm sitting here dicking around and all the girls are escaping!" He ran up the stairs in pursuit of the escaping girls. Apparently he netted one, because shortly thereafter, the band and road crew watched him head back into the Holiday Inn with her.

"Rivers just got here."

"Does he have some hot little number?"

"She's not really hot. She's not even Asian."

"Man, he's slipping."

Time passed and it became clear that Cuomo wasn't emerging from that hotel room. After a nervous phone call back to the West Coast management office, the road manager ultimately told the bus driver to move out. Cuomo made the show the following evening, but it required his buying a plane ticket to St. Louis.

● ● ●

Did Rod Stewart really get rushed to a hospital emergency room one night to get his stomach pumped after giving too many blow jobs?

No, no, no. Everybody knows that was Henry Kissinger!

There doesn't appear to be a whit of truth to the stomach-pump story, which was one of the best salacious rumors ever to circulate through a junior-high cafeteria. (And one of the most enduring—other names that have been attached to the story over the years include Jon Bon Jovi, Lil' Kim, and Britney Spears.) When asked about the rumor, the cheerfully bawdy Stewart has roared with laughter and said: "I was on my honeymoon with Alana in 1979 in Italy, and it was on the news that I'd been rushed to the hospital and they'd pumped out twelve pints. Can you imagine that? It must have been one after another! *C'mon, get your head down!* I firmly believe that a guy who used to work for me started the rumor."

● ● ●

I heard the Bee Gees wrote a bunch of their hit songs on the set of a porno movie. Can that be right?

The three Gibb brothers wrote most of their songs for the *Saturday Night Fever* soundtrack in a three-week-long marathon just outside Paris in 1977, holed up in the Château D'Hérouville Studio.

(The studio had previously hosted David Bowie, when he was recording *Pin Ups,* and Elton John, when he was making *Honky Chateau.*) Two years later Robin Gibb said, "There were so many pornographic films made at the Château. The staircase where we wrote 'How Deep Is Your Love,' 'Stayin' Alive,' all those songs, was the same staircase where there've been six classic lesbian porno scenes filmed. I was watching a movie one day called *Kinky Women of Bourbon Street,* and all of a sudden there's this château, and I said, 'It's *the* Château!' These girls, these dodgy birds, are having a scene on the staircase that leads from the front door up to the studio. There were dildos hangin' off the stairs and everything. I thought, '*Gawd,* we wrote "Night Fever" there!' "

> The Bee Gees contained twins Robin and the late Maurice Gibb; for some of the other twins in rock, see p. 92 in Chapter 6.

● ● ●

Did Mick Jagger write "Angie" for Angela Bowie to calm her down after she caught him and David Bowie in bed together?

Did they make the beast of burden with two backs? As Angela Bowie told the story (after her

post-divorce gag order expired), she came home
one morning in the '70s and found the "Dancing in
the Streets" duet partners in bed—naked but not
actually satisfying each other's every need. "I felt
absolutely dead certain that they'd been screw-
ing," she said. "I didn't have to look around for
open jars of KY Jelly." Jagger called her tale
"complete rubbish," while David Bowie declined
comment, saying in 1995, "About fifteen or
sixteen years ago, I really got pretty tired of
fending off questions about what I used to do with
my [penis] in the early seventies."

Angela says her blasé response to finding Mick
and David in bed was to make them breakfast, so
it seems unlikely that Jagger needed to calm her
down with a song. In addition, Keith Richards
says he wrote the 1973
ballad "Angie" without
Jagger; friends of
Richards say it was about
his girlfriend Anita
Pallenberg. (A competing
theory is that it's about
his daughter, but since
she was then known as
Dandelion, that seems
unlikely.) Describing how it was impossible for
Jagger to modify the lyrics, Richards said, "You try

> Mick Jagger's
> been in more than
> one celebrity's bed:
> Carly Simon's "You're
> So Vain" is often
> thought to be about
> him. For the full
> story, see p. 145 in
> Chapter 10.

and change it, man, and it never sounds right.
It's only two syllables, it could be 'bank note,'
but you always come back to 'Angie.' Once
you've put something together with a musical
phrase like that, it's like it's locked in, you never
pull it out."

● ● ●

I love Belle & Sebastian's album *The Boy with the Arab Strap*. But what's an Arab strap?

It's both a sex toy and a rock band. You want to
know about the sex toy, but I'm going to tell you
about the band first, anyway. Arab Strap is a
Scottish indie duo; their best album is probably
2001's *The Red Thread*. They started in 1995;
three years later, fellow Glaswegians Belle &
Sebastian paid them tribute with their album *The
Boy with the Arab Strap,* which is how people like
you first heard of the band (and the toy). Now
you're ready for the sex toy: "An Arab strap is
basically a cock ring of metal with two leather
straps. The ring goes around your dick and the
leather straps go around your balls and it keeps
you erect for longer," Malcolm Middleton, one-half
of Arab Strap, told me. He says their name came
from the band's singer, Aidan Moffett. "About ten
years ago, his girlfriend asked him to order a large

orange dildo from a magazine. And there was an offer: if you spent an extra five pounds on a video, I think it was called *Naked Werewolf Lady,* you got a free Arab strap." Moffett still has the original strap, which he carries around in his drum-machine case for good luck. Middleton said, "I believe he's not used it with anyone else, but he's tried it on a few times."

• • •

I've heard the stories about white panties, but I need the real deal—what did Elvis Presley like in bed?

One answer is "the costars of his movies." But the King loved to introduce the ladies to "Little Elvis," and many of them wrote tell-all books, so we know a fair bit about his preferences. Some of them are unsurprising: Presley liked girls who could give "great head," for example. Others confirm his status as a gentleman: His chosen method of birth control was to pull out and finish with his hand. And some of Presley's proclivities are legendary: He liked girls in lacy white panties, with some pubic hair coming out the sides. His biggest turnoff was women who were mothers; if he found out a girlfriend had ever had a baby, he lost all sexual interest in her.

As he got older, Presley sometimes just wanted a girl to sleep with—literally. He found it easier to fall asleep if there was a woman in bed with him. Presley preferred petite women, and he especially didn't want them to have large hands or feet. And although he was straight, Presley handled passes from gay men gracefully, usually turning them down by saying, "Hey, that just ain't my style."

• • •

What porn movie did the sample in 2 Live Crew's "Me So Horny" come from?

"Me so horny! Me love you long time!" promised a woman's voice on the 1990 rap single. Although actress Papillon Soo Soo sounded like she should be talking to Ron Jeremy in *Pretty Peaches 2,* she was actually speaking to Matthew Modine in *Full Metal Jacket.* (She played "Da Nang Hooker," who asked, "Hey, baby, you got girlfriend Vietnam?" Modine haggled, "Five dollars is all my mom allows me to spend.") While Stanley Kubrick's drama was nominated for an Academy Award, the 2 Live Crew single became the first record ever declared obscene in a United States court.

• • •

What's the story with Bebe Buell? Are Elvis Costello's late-'70s albums really about her?

These days, many people just know Bebe Buell as the mother of Liv Tyler, but in the '70s, she was a model and *Playboy* centerfold who had romantic liaisons with just about every major figure in rock, including Steven Tyler, Todd Rundgren, Iggy Pop, David Bowie, Mick Jagger, Jimmy Page, and Rod Stewart. "At the time, relations between models and rock stars were rare," she mused. "*Apres moi, le deluge.*" Buell was close enough to the Rolling Stones to report in her deliciously trashy autobiography, *Rebel Heart,* that Keith Richards was the best-endowed member of the group and that Jagger objected to her liaison with Steven Tyler, asking her, "Why do you want the fake Mick when you've got the real one?"

Buell certainly had an intense affair with Costello; as she described it, it lasted from 1978 to 1979, then again from 1982 to 1985, and ended when she aborted their child. She said he was the love of her life, and she saw their relationship as being a pervasive inspiration for Costello's work, down to the title of *Blood & Chocolate* (derived from her habit of demanding a candy bar whenever she got her period). Buell summarized: "It's scary what Elvis does. He writes these lyrics because he knows I will see them, but he also knows that if I try to express this to people, they will think I am nuts. He wants people to think I'm crazy; it delights him. *But deep down he knows the truth.*"

Costello, for his part, addressed Buell, although not by name, in the liner notes to a reissue of *Armed Forces:* "She turned up with eight pieces of luggage like a mail-order bride and moved in. I was too stupid and vain to resist. She'd later claim to have inspired most of the songs on this record—all of which were already written when we met. This was also said about the previous release—a chronological impossibility—and many of my other compositions to this day. It is a tragic delusion about which I wish I could say: 'I shall not dignify that with a response' but 'dignity' doesn't come into this story."

Buell called me up, objecting that she'd never claimed to be the inspiration for the songs on *Armed Forces*—which appears to be true. Although she's written about Costello using her life for inspiration in that period, and on the albums *Get Happy!* and *Blood & Chocolate* in particular, she seemed perfectly sane about where her influence upon him began and ended. Buell dismissed Costello's liner notes as more psychological gamesmanship. (And Costello's carefully crafted comment was not actually a denial of her influence on his life and music, although it certainly was intended to give that impression.) For all that, Buell has often seemed overeager to find any trace of her influence, to validate herself as muse rather than groupie. Take, for example, her contention about "Little Red Corvette": She believes that Prince wrote it about her, despite never having met her, and that he is actually singing "Bebe you're much too fast."

● ● ●

Who are the best-endowed male rock stars?

Since not every well-hung gentleman exposes himself on videotape like Tommy Lee did, and since I don't carry around a tape measure backstage, the people to consult on this question are groupies. And trading gossip online, they have reported that the following musicians are men of great repute: Chris Isaak, Robin Zander (Cheap Trick), Tony Kanal (No Doubt), Anthony Kiedis (Red Hot Chili Peppers), Jon Langford (the Mekons), Phil Anselmo (Pantera), Jerry Cantrell (Alice in Chains), John Dolmayan (System of a Down), and especially Huey Lewis. The late Jimi

> Okay, so that's what Jimi Hendrix had going on under his belt, but what about under his headband? The answer's on p. 150 of Chapter 11.

Hendrix, hugely talented in more than one way, was the prize in Cynthia Plaster Caster's collection of genital molds. And Iggy Pop's unit is so big it should have its own zip code. (Honorable mention goes to Sugar Ray's Mark McGrath, possibly the only rock star ever to brag about having a small penis.)

• • •

Was Marvin Gaye addicted to porn?

When Gaye died in 1984, people didn't put it that way—but the short answer would seem to be yes. Of course, Gaye's sexual proclivities were overshadowed by the circumstances of his death: Gaye was shot to death by his father, an apostolic preacher. Gaye had retreated to his parents' house to try to get clean, but he spent his final months periodically demanding cocaine and pornographic videotapes. For years, he had sought out smut in any format available—even postcards—with particular interest in S&M magazines and the European bondage cartoonist Georges Pichard. (He also recorded some notorious bootlegged tracks that his friends considered homemade pornography, such as 1979's sexual satire "Dem Niggers Are Savage in the Sack," not released during his lifetime, and 1983's "Sanctified Pussy"; both songs surfaced in sanitized posthumous versions on the 1985 collection *Dream of a Lifetime*.) When Gaye's biographer David Ritz visited his home in Ostend, Belgium, in 1982 and saw the collection of porn that Gaye had amassed, he told Gaye that he needed some "sexual healing"—providing the title for Gaye's last big hit single.

●　●　●

We've all seen the movie—is it true that the female backup singers for Ray Charles, the Raeletts, were called that because to be a Raelett, they had to "let Ray" have his way with them?

"That was a funny line, but not exactly true," Charles said when asked about that story. By his own admission, he slept with "many, many of the Raeletts" over the years, but he insisted that he had never strong-armed any of them into bed. "I'd never want to make love to a woman thinking that the only reason she agrees is because I'm her boss," he said.

Members of his band, however, said that when Charles was spurned by a woman, he could be exceptionally cruel to her, both offstage and on. One Raelett who turned down Charles's advances found herself humiliated onstage; when she hit a bum note during a concert, he played the section of the song she had muffed over and over, shouting "Repeat, repeat!" at her, while the audience laughed.

Charles added the Raeletts (originally called the Cookies) to his band in 1957; the call-and-response between him and the backup singers became a trademark element of his sound. "There was suddenly more perfume in the air," Charles said. That aroma led to Charles romancing many of the Raeletts, sometimes simultaneously, sometimes switching his affections from one to another. The seven other men in his band would also pursue whichever women Charles had spurned. Charles said he had no "policy against hanky-panky among the girls and boys in the band. How could I, as much as I loved to fuck?" Charles also loved to orchestrate orgies (or, as he called them, "parties"). "I don't like to conclude a day without female companionship," he confessed.

Charles also enjoyed the convenience of being able to sleep with his singers. "Don't get me wrong," he said. "If I was forced to look hard, I'd certainly look." Charles did have three rules for band romances, though: The music had to come first, hands off the underage girls, and no rough stuff. "I didn't put up with any fights where a chick might get hurt upside the head. I didn't want everyone in the band looking scratched or bruised with puffy eyes and swollen jaws. I didn't want the organization to look raunchy and tattered."

● ● ●

Is Bryan Adams's "Summer of '69" really about performing the sex act of 69?

Back in the summer of '85, Adams's nostalgic tale of his youth and his first rock band was a top-five hit: "I got my first real six-string / Bought it at the five-and-dime," Adams sang in "Summer of '69." Most people believed that he was referring to the year 1969; this was partially because of the apostrophe in the song's title, and partially because Adams was a clean-cut Canadian boy. If it had been a Prince song, there would have been less wholesome assumptions. But for anyone who did the math, the timeline was inescapable: Bryan Adams was only nine years old in the summer of 1969. This would have made him a tad young for the song's narrative, where his pal Jody gets married—either he was the world's most precocious third-grader or the title's apostrophe was just a fig leaf. Years later, Adams finally confirmed the dirty-minded suspicions: "That song always surprised me. From its inception it was always exciting, so I'm glad everyone else got it. One thing people never got, though, was the song isn't about the actual year 1969—it's about making love à la sixty-nine!"

• • •

I knew Bob Dylan and Joan Baez were lovers—but somebody told me she also had a fling with John Lennon! Is that true?

With more caffeine, it might have been. On consecutive nights circa 1964, both Baez and the Beatles performed at the Red Rocks Amphitheatre in Denver, Colorado. Baez had finished her tour, so when the Beatles invited her to tag along with them, she joined their entourage for a few concerts. "I saw all the inner workings: how you climb into Volkswagen buses and then send the limousine out to be beaten to death by loving fans," she said. After the tour, the Beatles ended up in a large mansion in L.A. "They've sent their people out to bring in groupies so they can pick who they're gonna, you know, hang out with. And these *poor girls,* just sitting downstairs waiting to see whether they're gonna be picked by somebody—they don't talk, they don't even *knit.*" There weren't enough bedrooms for everybody, so Lennon told Baez she could stay in his room.

"So I went to sleep and he came in, in the middle of the night," Baez said. "And I think he felt compelled—'Well, I've asked her and she is a star and *oh, dear* '—and he started coming on to me, very unenthusiastically. I said, 'John, you know, I'm probably as tired as you are, and I don't want you to feel you have to perform on my behalf.' And he says [in Liverpudlian accent], 'Oh, luvly! I mean, what a relief! Because you see, well, you might say I've already *been fooked* downstairs.' So we had a good laugh and went to sleep."

3

I HOLD
THE TITLE

And You Are the Challenger

My friend James used to have a simple litmus test with a band's debut album: If it was self-titled, he wouldn't buy it. His logic? If they were already out of ideas when it was time to name the record, why should he expect that they would have anything creative going on in their music? Strictly adhering to James's no-eponyms policy means you'll miss out on some great albums, of course (*The Clash, Van Halen, Run-D.M.C., The Velvet Underground & Nico*), but his point remains: When it comes to songs and albums, titles can range from the mundane to the sublime to the ridiculous. *You* decide which category "Rainy Day Women #12 & 35" falls into.

● ● ●

Who or what is Jane in the title of Maroon 5's album *Songs About Jane*? Is it a drug reference?

"Jane is my ex-girlfriend," Adam Levine, Maroon 5's lead singer, told me. "I wanted to name the record really sincerely—record names are so clever and cute these days. I was eighteen or nineteen when I saw Jane at the gas station, and I fell in love with her. I sweet-talked her, made her fall in love with me, then I got frustrated with her and we parted ways." How does Jane feel about having a hit album named after her? "I actually asked her permission," Levine said. "That was the last time we spoke. She seemed flattered, but I know she disapproves of me and what I do with my life."

● ● ●

Where did Pink Floyd's *Atom Heart Mother* get its name?

Pink Floyd's symphonic fourth album remained
untitled until the band was debuting some of the
material on the BBC's Radio 1—and the announcer
needed to call it *something*. Album producer Ron
Geesin told bassist Roger Waters to search
through a copy of the
Evening Standard, a
London newspaper that
was lying around the
studio. Waters spotted an
article about a pregnant
woman with an atomic-powered pacemaker and
borrowed its ATOM HEART MOTHER headline.

Never heard of
Pink Floyd's *Household
Objects* album? Find
out why on p. 165 of
Chapter 12.

• • •

Did Chic's "Le Freak"
originally have a different title?

Yes. Guitarist Nile Rodgers was irate that he was
turned away from the nightclub Studio 54, even
though his band's hit song "Dance, Dance, Dance
(Yowsah, Yowsah, Yowsah)" was playing within.
So he wrote a song about it. The chorus? "Aww,
fuck off!"

"I'm a former Black Panther," Rodgers told me,
"but Bernard [Edwards, Chic's bassist] was
religious." So they compromised. "Freak off" was
watered-down and lame, but when they changed

Bernard Edwards, the man, the myth, the legend: The story of his finest moment is on p. 167 of Chapter 12.

it to "Aww, freak out!" they had a song that would spend five weeks at number one in 1978, and establish Rodgers and Edwards as the preeminent producers of disco. Needless to say, Rodgers didn't have any trouble getting into Studio 54 after that.

● ● ●

What exactly does the title of Radiohead's album *Kid A* refer to?

One early theory upon the album's 2000 release was that the title was borrowed from "Kid A in Alphabet Land," a collection of trading cards about French psychoanalyst Jacques Lacan, whose theories helped inspire postmodernism. Singer Thom Yorke quickly debunked that, but encouraged speculation that the title referred to the first genetically cloned child. "I'm sure somewhere it's been done, even though it's illegal now," he said. Since the album was full of electronic treatments of Yorke's voice, this inspired theorizing about the hidden architecture of the album being replicated DNA. The true inspiration was a bit more mundane, however; "Kid A" was a bit of studio technology—a software program of children's voices that ended up not making the album's final mix. If a different sequencer or synth setting had caught the group's eye, their fourth album might have been called "Tenor Sax" or "Ocarina."

What's that guy saying in Radiohead's "Just" video? See p. 15 of Chapter 1.

• • •

I've always wanted to know—what does the title of the Beatles' "Norwegian Wood" mean, anyway? Is it an IKEA reference?

No, that would be *Swedish* wood. According to John Lennon, the sitar-inflected "Norwegian Wood (This Bird Has Flown)" was about an affair he was having. (Lennon was routinely unfaithful to his first wife, Cynthia.) The title comes after the narrator has had an unconsummated evening with a girl and goes to sleep in the bath at two A.M. He wakes up alone and sings, "So I lit a fire, isn't it good, Norwegian wood." Lennon said he wrote the song by himself—" 'Norwegian Wood' is my song completely"—but soon before his death in 1980, he expressed bafflement about the song's title, saying "I don't know *how* the hell I got to 'Norwegian Wood.' "

Paul McCartney, however, said *he* knew—because he came up with the title himself. In 1965, McCartney was living in an upstairs room in the home of the Asher family in London, which he found a most congenial arrangement: He enjoyed all the domestic comforts of home; he saw his girlfriend, actress Jane Asher, on a regular basis; and he spent hours hanging out with her brother, Peter Asher (of the folk duo Peter and Gordon). "Peter Asher had his room done out in wood; a lot of people were decorating their places in wood. Norwegian wood. It was pine really, cheap pine. But it's not as good a title, 'Cheap Pine.' "

So although Lennon thought the song was all his, McCartney remembers it as a collaboration; from his perspective, the affair was completely imaginary, so he felt free to embellish the girl's home with inexpensive wood panels. Discussing the song's ending, McCartney said that he and Lennon identified with the spurned narrator: "In our world, the guy had to have some sort of revenge. It could have meant 'I lit a fire to keep myself warm, and wasn't the décor of her house wonderful?' But it didn't, it meant 'I burned the fucking place down as an act of revenge.' "

In 1965, the Beatles also got their MBEs. What the hell's an MBE? See p. 7 in Chapter 1.

• • •

What's up with all these double Rs in the titles of pop songs? "Hot in Herre" by Nelly? "Right Thurr" by Chingy? "Dirrty" by Christina Aguilera?

"That's just how we talk!" Chingy said when I asked him. "In California, they say it proper." Chingy is from St. Louis, as is Nelly, and says that the extra R is an effort to represent the local accent. (Aguilera isn't from thurr, which means either that she's latching on to an urban trend or that her song title is one more mystery for Christina's world.) Chingy tried to pronounce *there* in the style he called "proper"—so it rhymes with *hair* instead of *her*—but could barely get it out of his mouth. After a few attempts, he gave up and said, "I can't even say it like that, it'd sound stupid."

• • •

I have looked far and wide for the meaning of the title to Guns N' Roses' *"The Spaghetti Incident?"*—please enlighten me!

"It's a very silly story," warned Duff McKagan (formerly the bassist for Guns N' Roses, now a member of Velvet Revolver) when I asked. The title has its origins in the summer of 1989, when singer Axl Rose wanted the band to relocate to Chicago. "The idea was Axl was from over the border in Indiana and he wanted to be close to home. So we got two condos and rehearsed above the Metro, and Axl never showed up."

While McKagan, guitarist Slash, and drummer Steven Adler were waiting for Rose, they wrote a bunch of songs for *Use Your Illusion* and ate a lot of Italian takeout. "And Steven was doing a lot of crack cocaine at this point, and he'd keep his blow in the refrigerator. So his code word for his stash was *spaghetti*," McKagan told me. "Steven spiraled out of control. We said, Steven, *we're* fucked-up individuals and we're telling you that you gotta shape up, so you must be *really* fucked up." Adler was fired in July 1990, the first member of the group to get canned (placing him years ahead of the GN'R curve).

Adler then sued the band under the novel premise that his drug addiction was their fault. While giving a deposition for the 1993 trial, McKagan was asked to cite instances of Adler's bad behavior; he mentioned the Chicago drug stash. "So then I'm in court, with a jury and the whole thing, and this fuckin' lawyer gets up, and with a straight face says, 'Mr. McKagan, tell us about the spaghetti incident.' And I started laughing." The band ultimately settled out of court, writing Adler a check for two and a half million dollars. When McKagan read through the trial transcripts, he was struck by the straight-faced absurdity of the phrase "the spaghetti incident," which is how it ended up as an album title (complete with quotation marks) later that year.

You may have also wondered about the small semaphore message on the bottom of the cover of *"The Spaghetti Incident?"* McKagan never even noticed it was there; Slash peered at it and then told me, "It does have a meaning, but I've forgotten what." Only Axl Rose knows what it means now, and he's not talking.

Another very silly story about Guns N' Roses involves Depeche Mode and "shooting pigs for fun"; see p. 116 of Chapter 9.

4 LAWYERS, GUNS, AND MONEY

Mysteries of the Music Business and the Pop Charts

I've been writing feature articles about musicians for about two decades now, starting with my college rock magazine, *Nadine* (named after the Chuck Berry song and edited by a crew of friends who are still among the coolest people I've ever known). My first interview: They Might Be Giants ("Wow, you really know our material," John Linnell said. "If I had known that, I wouldn't have lied so much.") The first interview I got paid for: A short *Spin* profile of Bad English, the now-forgotten fusion of John Waite and Journey's

Neal Schon, who had a number one single with "When I See You Smile." ("Is it too Keith Richards?" Waite asked me as he tied a scarf around his ankle. Even though it was my first time backstage, I knew instinctively that of the many problems that afflicted his ankle scarf, an excess of Keithness was not among them.) The interview that got me a job at *Details:* J. Mascis of Dinosaur Jr. (no pithy quote in this parenthesis—he just grunted at me a lot and crushed peanuts the whole time we spoke).

Anyway, the point of this chapter introduction is not that I used my access to the music world to answer a lot of the questions in this book (although that's true) or that I can use these introductions to tell self-indulgent war stories if I feel like it (also true). The point is this: A lot's changed about the music business in the past twenty years, and I am now a well-informed observer instead of a bewildered outsider wondering what exactly a "mechanical royalty" is, anyway. But one thing has remained constant: If a record company can screw a young act, they will.

● ● ●

Why are CDs released on Tuesdays?

"We decided to level the playing field back in the mid-eighties," Joe McFadden, senior vice president of sales and field marketing at Capitol Records, informed me. "Records used to come out 'the week of,' and retailers would sell it when they got it." This created some serious discrepancies; stores that were more remote geographically, or that had a longer distribution chain, would get the music much later. So the labels settled on Tuesdays as a universal release date. "We were trying to avoid anyone breaking the street date," McFadden said. "We figured if people got the product on Monday, they could sell it on Tuesday. And even if distributors got it on Friday, they couldn't get it on sale in stores over the weekend." This also had the advantage of getting people to visit record stores on a steady schedule—although recently, rush releases of leaked records have happened on other days. And, McFadden confided, "There have been backroom conversations among labels recently about moving the street date to Friday."

● ● ●

Help me settle a bet! A

friend of mine insists that Billy Ocean had exactly three number one hits—and that all of them had exactly eight words in the title. I say that can't possibly be right: "When the Going Gets Tough, the Tough Get Going" obviously has nine words in the title!

Indeed it does—which is perhaps the reason that song fell short of the number one slot, hitting number two in 1985. Strange as it may seem, your friend wins the bet. Billy Ocean, the likeable singer of pop songs lightly inflected with reggae, hit the top of the charts exactly three times; each time the complete song title had exactly eight words in it. Let the Freemasons ponder these twenty-four words of mystical power: "Caribbean Queen (No More Love on the Run)," "There'll Be Sad Songs (To Make You Cry)," "Get Outta My Dreams, Get into My Car."

● ● ●

Sometimes I'll see an import release by one of my favorite bands in my local record store with two or more extra songs on it. Why do the foreign releases get so many extras?

"Eighty percent of those import releases come from Japan," John Voigtmann, senior director of international marketing at RCA Records, told me. "By law, Japan's music industry is artifically divided into two categories, and import CDs are always sold at cheaper prices than local editions. So, in order for Japanese companies to stay competitive, we provide them with extra tracks. Anything other than that is usually a special marketing campaign; we might add some 'live in Norway' tracks to make it cool for Norwegians." Of course, many foreign releases are exactly the same as the American versions—but your local store doesn't bother to import those.

● ● ●

What song has been covered the most?

Unfortunately, the major song-rights organizations, ASCAP and BMI, don't keep track of this data—they're more concerned with how many times a song is played than by how many different people. But by general agreement, the song in the rock era with the most cover versions is "Yesterday," a Lennon/ McCartney composition. (Or, as Sir Paul would prefer it, given that he wrote it all by himself, a McCartney/Lennon composition.) It's been put on wax by more than two thousand different performers, including

For more information on a different Lennon/McCartney composition— "Norwegian Wood (This Bird Has Flown)"—see p. 47 in Chapter 3.

Ray Charles, En Vogue, Marvin Gaye, Merle Haggard, Elvis Presley, LeAnn Rimes, the Supremes, Tammy Wynette, and a whole bunch of different elevator-music string sections. The Gershwin ballad "Summertime," from *Porgy & Bess,* however, seems to have even more versions than that; and "Silent Night," written by Josef Mohr and Franz Gruber in 1818, may come in as many as five thousand different versions on various records.

● ● ●

Did James Brown really fine his musicians if he wasn't happy with their performance?

Absolutely; the hardest-working man in show business couldn't put on a show with the military precision of his '60s revue without being a tough boss. Bobby Byrd, who sang backup vocals for Brown as one of the Famous Flames, gave me the details. He said that Brown's fines were usually five or ten dollars, but they went up dramatically when he was

Another soul genius had strict, but very different, rules of the road for his legendary revue; see p. 37 in Chapter 2 for the regulations of Ray Charles.

playing at the Apollo Theater in 1962, where he was recording a live album: fifty or a hundred dollars for a miscue. Byrd told me, "James would do a routine when he fined you, counting off that hundred dollars. You'd whisper on the stage, 'Man, get your part right,' and then he'd see you and fine you for carrying on a conversation."

● ● ●

Before Nelly did it with "Dilemma" and "Hot in Herre," who was the last recording artist to simultaneously have both the number one and number two songs on the Billboard Top 100?

Not many people noticed, but Ja Rule did it in March 2002. "Ain't It Funny," by Jennifer Lopez featuring Ja Rule, was number one, while "Always on Time," by Ja Rule featuring Ashanti, was number two. If you sneer at guest appearances, then the last act to qualify was the Bee Gees in 1978, with "Night Fever" and "Stayin' Alive." Only four other acts in the rock era had occupied the top two slots simultaneously before Nelly: P. Diddy, Boyz II Men, Elvis Presley, and the Beatles (who had the top *five* singles the first week of April 1964: from top to bottom, they were

"Can't Buy Me Love," "Twist and Shout," "She Loves You," "I Want to Hold Your Hand," and "Please Please Me").

● ● ●

Everyone knows John Lennon and Paul McCartney signed a bad songwriting contract while in the Beatles. George Harrison, however, never complained about any ownership problems with his songs. Was he bound to a different contract?

Lennon and McCartney were perpetually unhappy with Northern Songs, their publishing company—largely because they felt they had been jobbed out of 51 percent of the ownership by Dick James before they got savvy to the ways of music publishing. "We could see owning a house, a guitar, or a car; they were physical objects," McCartney said. "But a song, not being a physical object, we couldn't see how it was possible to have a copyright in it. And therefore, with great glee, publishers saw us coming."

Harrison, however, had it even worse whenever Northern Songs handled one of his compositions; although he was contractually bound to the company and received royalties for songs he wrote, his percentage ownership in Northern was tiny. Originally he owned no part of the company, but when it went public in 1965 he and Ringo Starr each bought a whopping one-half of one percent of the shares. (Lennon and McCartney were issued 20 percent each.) So Harrison did, indeed, bellyache. "Only a Northern Song," his contribution to the soundtrack of *Yellow Submarine*, laid out his complaint: "It doesn't really matter what chords I play . . . it's only a Northern Song." Harrison's Northern Songs contract lapsed in 1968; he briefly signed with Apple Publishing and then started his own publishing company, Singsong Ltd., later renamed Harrisongs.

● ● ●

I heard my CDs will disintegrate after twenty or thirty years—is that true?

If compact discs self-destructed after twenty years, then the earliest discs would be vanishing in puffs of digital smoke right about now—and they're not. But despite the early marketing claims of "perfect sound forever," a few small batches are already unplayable; some defective late-'80s discs manufactured in the U.K. suffered from "CD rot," where the top layer puckered and the contents oxidized. "Those things are pancakes, and in the end, they're going to pop apart,"

I was told by Ted Sheldon, chair of the Audio Engineering Society's standards committee on preservation and restoration of audio. "It's an open question as to when. I think most CDs, if kept inside and out of the sun, should last for fifty years. But I don't know that—there hasn't been enough accelerated life testing." CD-Rs probably will have even shorter life spans because the laser you burn them with at home is less powerful than one found in commercial models. Of course, even if your CDs survive for decades, you'll need to maintain the right equipment—when was the last time you tried to play a 78-rpm record?

● ● ●

On their album *Last Splash,* the Breeders cover a song called "Invisible Man." I've looked everywhere, but I can't discover who wrote it. You're my only hope—do you know who wrote the song?

The *Last Splash* CD is strangely lacking in songwriting credits, but according to BMI, which supervises the band's publishing, the song's sole author is Kim Deal, leader of the Breeders. Perhaps you're thinking of "Drivin' on 9," the only cover on *Last Splash,* originally performed by the quirky folk-calypso band Ed's Redeeming Qualities; Ed's violinist, Carrie Bradley, has sometimes played with the Breeders. Other songs covered by the Breeders on disc include the Beatles' "Happiness Is a Warm Gun," the Who's "So Sad About Us," Hank Williams's "I Can't Help It (If I'm Still in Love with You)," Aerosmith's "Lord of the Thighs," and the theme from *Buffy the Vampire Slayer.*

● ● ●

Who had the most number two singles without hitting number one?

En Vogue had three singles that fell just short, as did Blood, Sweat & Tears, but the champion of silver medals on the Billboard Hot 100, without a doubt, was Creedence Clearwater Revival, who had five number two singles, all of them between March 1969 and October 1970: "Proud Mary," "Bad Moon Rising," "Green River," "Travelin' Band," and "Lookin' out My Back Door." (That falls short of the record for the most number two singles ever, which belongs to Madonna, with six; of course, she has a dozen number one singles to go along with them.) Bandleader John Fogerty was philosophical about not making it to the top of the pops, saying, "Number two tries harder and all that."

● ● ●

Did Neil Young really buy 150,000 copies of his own *Comes a Time* just so he could destroy them?

Nope—Young bought *200,000* copies. Young, as is his habit, tinkered with *Comes a Time* until its release, switching around the running order and also repeatedly changing album covers. Then, just before the release, he discovered that he had approved a test pressing of the record made from a damaged master tape—some of the high frequencies were missing. When Young alerted his record company, he discovered that they had already printed 200,000 copies and shipped them around the world. He acknowledged that it was his mistake but insisted on recalling the records; his bill was over $160,000. "I don't like throwing money around," he told his father. "But I wasn't going to have this album circulating around the world in bad quality." How did Young guarantee that the recalled records wouldn't leak out? He kept the cases of albums on his ranch—after firing at each box with a rifle.

I'M WITH THE BAND

Groupies

Any romantic notion of groupies as sexual pioneers dissipated decades ago, but I've certainly seen them hanging around backstage, making eyes at the boys in the band. There was that foxy blond in Arizona who was wearing overalls and panties, and nothing else, showing off a lot of tanned skin for the boys in Social Distortion. There were the girls hanging around outside the *Daily Show* studio, waiting to meet Third Eye Blind's singer, Stephan Jenkins.

When they complained they couldn't get backstage at concerts, Jenkins told them that they could if they really wanted to, but declined to explain how. The secret answer, of course, was "suck off a roadie or three." Some bands in recent years aren't particularly pleased by the notion of their fans buying backstage access with their bodies, but most don't lay down the law with the road crew, for fear of a mutiny in the ranks. That's why I once saw a roadie at an arena concert with a pertinent *USA Today* article clipped and pasted inside his flight case: STATUTORY RAPE: A LOOK AT LAWS STATE BY STATE.

● ● ●

What ever happened to the Plaster Casters?

"The world of plaster is a crazy one," confided the woman who would know, Cynthia Plaster Caster. In case you're not familiar with her oeuvre, she became famous for making casts of the penises of rock stars. She had a variety of female accomplices, who concentrated on the job of keeping the star stimulated. "I've always been the mold mixer," Plaster Caster told me. "This backfired on my original intent, which was to get laid." The Chicago native has accumulated an eclectic collection of units since 1968, including Jello

Biafra (the Dead Kennedys), Wayne Kramer (the MC5), and Jimi Hendrix.

Plaster Caster endured an ugly court case in the early '90s over ownership of her molds, which she won (although some of the plaster originals are gone forever, she has bronze copies). She's still mixing plaster today—some of her recent acquisitions include David Yow of the Jesus Lizard and Suzi Gardner of L7 (she's added boobs to her repertoire). Plaster Caster has also started a nonprofit foundation for non-mainstream artists; to raise money, she's selling limited editions of some of her casts, including the Hendrix monolith. (For more information, see www.cynthiapcaster .org.) And she's teaching classes for couples, which come with a plaster-casting diploma. "It's bizarre to have people tell me I'm a legend," said the cheerful Plaster Caster. "I think it's time to pass on the gauntlet before it's too late."

● ● ●

Who is "the Butter Queen" mentioned in the Rolling Stones song "Rip This Joint"?

The Butter Queen, real name Barbara Cope, was an industrious groupie based in Dallas, Texas, who was linked with countless '70s rock stars from Joe Cocker to Donovan to Mick Jagger. "I got on with her famously," Elton John said. David Cassidy has described her showing up at his hotel suite in the early '70s with two apprentices, ready to orally service his entire band and crew. She called room service and ordered her trademark: a pound of butter. She used the Land O'Lakes as a lubricant, but of course, once it warmed up it smelled like hot popcorn—which meant that a blow job from the Butter Queen had the distinctly unerotic aroma of a movie theater's lobby.

● ● ●

Who is the "Sweet Connie" in Grand Funk Railroad's "We're an American Band"?

Connie Hamzy was a diligent groupie in Little Rock, Arkansas; starting as a teenager in the early '70s, she screwed just about every rock star who came through town—she especially liked drummers—and lots of their roadies, too. ("Sweet, sweet Connie, doin' her act / She had the whole show and that's a natural fact," Grand Funk sang. Possibly in tribute to Hamzy's preferences, the vocals were taken by Don Brewer, who was, yes, the band's drummer.) Among the partners she claims in *Rock Groupie,* her unpublished autobiography: Keith Moon (who once used a banana),

John Bonham, Mick Fleetwood, Richard Carpenter, Huey Lewis, Alice Cooper, Rick Springfield, Waylon Jennings, Doc Severinsen, and Don Henley and Glenn Frey (at the same time). She also reports being propositioned by then-governor Bill Clinton (which he's denied); she says she was willing, but they couldn't find a room. When Hamzy began publicizing her hobby, she had to go to court to keep her job as a school-teacher; she's also unsuccessfully run for Congress and for mayor of Little Rock. In her book, she says that the secret to success as a groupie is being willing to service a dozen roadies before you get to the band: "At concerts, almost every girl in the first twenty rows secretly hopes that somehow, through the smoke and lights, she will be spotted from the stage and summoned to a band member's bed. Things rarely happen that way. By the time the band goes on, I'm either astride a speaker onstage or a crew member out back."

● ● ●

Is it true that Led Zeppelin caught a fish and then incorporated it into sex play with a groupie?

If you're a young rock band, you have to face up to the humbling realization that whenever you're considering an illegal or immoral act, there's a good chance Led Zeppelin did it first. As Zep's road manager, Richard Cole, told the story, the band liked to stay at the Edgewater Inn in Seattle: It was right on the Puget Sound, and they could fish out of their window. In July 1969, he and drummer John Bonham spent a drunken night reeling in fish. The next day, with the dead fish still floating in the wastebasket, the band was hanging out in the room, entertaining some girls. One of them, "Jackie, a tall redhead from Portland, seventeen years old," was swigging champagne from the bottle and telling the group how much she enjoyed being tied up during sex. Determined to oblige her, Cole wrote, he tied her to the bed, told her "I'm putting this red snapper in your red snapper," and made good on his word.

"That's totally wrong," Carmine Appice (drummer for Vanilla Fudge, who employed Cole before Zeppelin did) told me. "It was *my* groupie." Both bands were in town for the Seattle Pop Festival, and Appice was hanging out in Zep bassist John Paul Jones's room with the girl and Fudge keyboard player Mark Stein, who had an 8mm camera. "She saw the camera, and kept

saying she wanted to play around." Then Bonham
and two members of Fudge's road crew invaded
the room with the catch of the day: a mud shark,
not a snapper. "We moved to my room, and it got
pretty gross. I decided to leave, and then I realized
I was in my room already." At various points, most
of Zeppelin and the Fudge came in for a look at the
groupie being pleasured with the shark. Singer
Robert Plant of Led Zeppelin recently confirmed
that while he saw some of the proceedings, it was
really a Vanilla Fudge event. Appice told me that
Cole made up the name "Jackie": "In those days,
Richard was so out of it, I'm surprised he remembers his own name." Surprisingly, Frank Zappa
got more of the details right in his song "Mud-
shark."

Appice has kept drumming with acts such as
Rod Stewart and Pink Floyd; he's currently playing
with a reformed Vanilla
Fudge and working on an
autobiography, *The
International Rock Guide
to Hotel Wrecking*. Randy
Pratt, who ended up with
the 8mm film of the
incident, recently tried to
develop it, only to

The other great
Led Zeppelin mystery,
of course, is what the
symbols on the cover
of their fourth album
mean. Turn to p. 211
of Chapter 15 for some
answers.

discover that it was too old. The Edgewater Inn is still in business; rooms on the water side recently went for $259 per night and up. Although the hotel's Web site has featured a photo of the Beatles fishing from their window, for some reason it omits any mention of Led Zeppelin or Vanilla Fudge.

6 | I'M IN THE BAND

The Second Drummer Drowned

There's nobody quieter in an interview than a replacement member of a band: the studio assistant who got the job as guitarist because the singer noticed he could play the licks better than the actual guitarist; the bassist who got drafted when the rest of the band decided they couldn't take one more bus ride with that founding member. And there's nobody louder than a lead singer who's decided to say how he really feels about a departed member of the group. The smart ones take the dignified high road, even when that drummer was a substance-abusing freak who was bringing down the whole band—but who ever said lead singers were smart?

• • •

Did Chevy Chase play drums for Steely Dan?

Not really. As Donald Fagen has put it: "We went to college with Chevy and before we ever thought of the idea of Steely Dan we used to do pickup dates with Chevy on drums. He was a very good drummer." Let's fill that statement in with some more detail. The institution in question was Bard College, in upstate New York, in the late '60s. Fagen led a band that cycled through a variety of names, including the Don Fagen Jazz Trio, the Bad Rock Group, and the Leather Canary. (Before you snort in derision at that last name, ask yourself if Steely Dan is really that much of an improvement, nomenclaturally.) Fagen recruited Walter Becker, two years younger, after hearing him play blues guitar in a student lounge; Chase was one of a variety of drummers who filled out that group.

But a bunch of things would happen before Becker and Fagen started Steely Dan: They would leave Bard in 1969 (Fagen graduating, Becker not), peddle songs at the Brill Building (they did manage to place one of their songs, "I Mean to Shine," on a Barbra Streisand album), play as backing musicians on a tour with Jay & the Americans, and move to Los Angeles. Only then, more than two years after they left Bard, did Steely Dan start. So while Chevy Chase earned himself a footnote in rock history, he was in Steely Dan the way that a guy who played washtub in the Quarrymen, Lennon and McCartney's teenage skiffle group, was in the Beatles. Or as Becker and Fagen might say: They're Steely Dan, and he's not.

For information on Steely Dan versus the Eagles, best two falls out of three, see p. 103 of Chapter 8.

● ● ●

Who was originally supposed to be the vocalist of the Sex Pistols?

In the first version of the Pistols, before the band had even decided on a name, Steve Jones was the singer. In the spring of 1975, they pushed out founder Wally Nightingale, and Jones moved over to guitar. Malcolm McLaren suggested various candidates for the vacant frontman slot, including Johnny Thunders and Sylvain Sylvain (both of the New York Dolls), Richard Hell (of Television), and

Midge Ure (who went on to be the lead singer of Ultravox). In August '75, John Lydon (later known as Johnny Rotten) walked into McLaren's boutique, Sex, and got the job with a lip-synching performance. "I knew practically none of the records inside Malcolm's jukebox because it was all that awful sixties mod music that I couldn't stand," Lydon said. "The only song I could cope with was Alice Cooper's 'Eighteen.' I just gyrated like a belly dancer."

For some other historically important moments in rock 'n' roll dancing, check out p. 79 of this very chapter.

• • •

Has any band been together with all its founding members longer than U2 has?

Forming in 1978 at Mount Temple High School in Dublin, the four members of U2 have now spent an extraordinary twenty-eight years together (as of 2006). But UB40 has kept an eight-man lineup for just as long, while Los Lobos clock in at thirty-three years, and ZZ Top at thirty-six. The best way to guarantee that a band acts like a family, though, is to actually be one: The Osmonds had approximately twenty-five uninterrupted years together, while the Neville Brothers have twenty-nine years together (and counting). Barry, Maurice, and Robin Gibb, however, started performing as the Bee Gees in 1958, which means they logged forty-five years of improbably high-pitched harmonies before Maurice's death in 2003.

● ● ●

Okay, if D12 isn't Eminem's band, how did they hook up?

The late rapper Proof, Eminem's friend and rap-battle mentor, started the group around 1995; the idea was to create a free-floating group of all-star rappers, the Detroit version of the Wu-Tang Clan. The name stood for both Detroit Twelve and Dirty Dozen. The MCs thought the group would have a Western theme, like a gang of outlaw horsemen—but when they rented *The Dirty Dozen,* they found it was actually a World War II movie. Effectively doubling the group's six rappers into a dozen, Proof decided that everyone in D12 should have a doppelgänger identity. He said, "The whole thing in D12 was to have a personality where you would just say anything. You just didn't give a fuck. Your persona was almost like a mask to hide behind, know what I'm sayin'?" Eminem was the last one

Eminem would soon hook up with Dr. Dre; get the story on page 119 of Chapter 9.

to come up with that kind of mask, but it proved to be worth the wait. In 1997, sitting on the toilet—no, really—he invented the nihilistic Slim Shady identity. "Em took Slim Shady and he ran with it," Proof said. "He took it way more serious than all of us, that motherfucker."

● ● ●

Why did the Clash throw Mick Jones out of the band?

By the end, those guys couldn't *stand* each other. When the Clash made *Combat Rock,* Jones and Joe Strummer couldn't even be in the studio at the same time; Jones worked during the day, while Strummer took the night shift. There were also genuine musical differences: Jones wanted funk, while Strummer preferred punk. But primarily, Jones resented how Strummer took control of the band, while Strummer and bassist Paul Simonon were tired of Jones behaving like a rock star— demanding that a cigarette be placed in his mouth before he went onstage, for example. When drummer Topper Headon quit in 1983, Jones lost his last ally in the group. Jones said, "We all knew that we were just doing it for the money. We couldn't face each other. In rehearsals we'd all look at the floor." As Strummer told it, "Mick eventually said, 'I don't mind what the Clash does, as long as you check it with my lawyer first.' I said, 'Go and write songs with your lawyer. Piss off!' "

Did Joe Strummer run a marathon in a chicken suit? See p. 18 of Chapter 1.

● ● ●

Why does Bez get a credit on Happy Mondays recordings?

That question has a surprising answer, but a few words of explanation may be in order first, for those who don't remember the Happy Mondays (i.e., most Americans). They were a dance/rock band, huge in England circa 1990, with singles like "Step On" and "Kinky Afro," and famed for their offstage destruction and prodigious consumption of drugs. Their anthem "24 Hour Party People" was used as the title of an amazing 2002 movie about the Manchester rock scene. (Seriously, rent it.) One member, "Bez" (born Mark Berry), didn't play a musical instrument; during gigs, he would do pop-eyed, spastic karate dancing. On albums, Bez was usually credited with "percussion, freaky dancing"; sometimes, "bezness" was added to that list of contributions. After the Happy Mondays broke up, lead singer Shaun Ryder started another group in the same mode, Black Grape. Ryder didn't play any musical instruments himself; when the one Monday he chose to join him in Black Grape was Bez, the other nonmusical member of the group, everyone wondered if it was a cunning plan or a cosmic joke.

So the surprising answer as to why Bez gets a credit for dancing is that he made the band better. I can testify from personal experience: I never saw the Happy Mondays play, but I did travel to England in 1995 to interview Black Grape. The part of my story where I followed Ryder around while he scored drugs isn't so pertinent here; nor is Ryder's anecdote about smashing into a clergyman's car with his Audi and fleeing the scene, only to discover that he had left his license plate behind at the site of the accident. What *is* relevant is that I saw Black Grape rehearse (until Ryder lost interest, which didn't take long). At the beginning of the rehearsal, when the band was milling around aimlessly, Bez showed himself to be musically knowledgeable, offering his opinions on what kind of wah-wah guitar would best suit the song. When Black Grape first ran through the song ("Big Day in the North"), it sounded stiff and clunky, not together. But then Bez started dancing, and the music improved dramatically. I don't think this is just because I had something entertaining to watch: the grave-faced Bez grooving from side to side with his arms akimbo, looking like James Coburn doing the Funky Chicken. No, I'd say it was partially because the other musicians found him inspiring, and mostly because he was marking out the beat with his body, giving them a visual focus that produced a musical groove.

This isn't without precedent—Charlie Watts legendarily picked up the Rolling Stones' backbeat from the movements of Mick Jagger's ass. But Bez proved to be a trendsetter. In the mid-'90s, Hazel, an indie-rock band from Portland, Oregon, had dancer Fred Nemo as a full member; he added extra comic

Mick Jagger got his ass out of the London School of Economics once the Rolling Stones got a record deal—but what were his grades before he dropped out? See p. 203 of Chapter 15.

value by dressing in costume, doing handstands onstage, and generally looking like a lumberjack. For some inexplicable reason, Mick Jagger's ass never got a credit of its own on a Rolling Stones album, so let us nod in its general direction as we salute Bez's pioneering ways.

BLOOD ON BLOOD

Rock 'n' Roll Families

The most violent, explosive running feuds in rock bands are often between brothers: Ray and Dave Davies of the Kinks, Chris and Rich Robinson of the Black Crowes, Noel and Liam Gallagher of Oasis. It makes sense if you think about it: If you're the leader of a successful group, your world is groupies, peeled grapes, and color-sorted M&Ms. But while everybody around you, down to the drummer, is deferring to you and your artistic whims, there's one guy in the band who not only isn't snapping to attention, he knows exactly what to say to wind you up. And *that's* how fights start onstage.

● ● ●

Does Steven Tyler ever find himself inappropriately attracted to his daughter Liv?

That's one of those questions you save for the end of an interview, in case the guy gets offended and hangs up the phone. But when I asked Tyler, the Aerosmith singer replied, "Oh, absolutely," adding his trademark cackle. "How can a father not be attracted to his daughter, especially when she's a cross between the girl he married and himself? Unless he's an ugly man, a father is always gonna be sexually attracted to his daughter on a certain level." So you're saying incest is based in vanity? "Positively, there's a certain level of narcissism in incest. All a man has to do is be totally honest with himself and he can see it. However, the real man knows that's just a place to never go. Instead he celebrates it by telling his daughter how beautiful she is and what a precious child of God she is. There's ways to love it without making love to it—I wrote 'Janie's Got a Gun' about fathers who don't know the difference."

● ● ●

Is Brian Eno royalty?

Eno's full name has deceived some people into thinking there's noble blood in the family: The superstar producer was christened Brian Peter George St John le Baptiste de la Salle Eno. But he's a commoner with a British father and a Belgian mother. When his father, William Eno, was serving in the British army during World War II, he stayed in a Belgian household and fell in love with a photo of the family's daughter, who was building airplanes in a Nazi forced-labor camp. At war's end, she returned weighing only seventy pounds, but alive, and William successfully wooed her. Back in England, Eno's father worked as a mailman—as did his uncle, grandfather, and great-grandfather. As Eno has drily noted, he comes from "a long line of people in the communications field."

● ● ●

Is Hank Williams Jr. really Kid Rock's father?

No, but they're friends and collaborators—and Williams has jokingly called Rock his "rebel son."

(Williams also has a biological rebel son, the country-punk Hank Williams III.) When Rock first met his hero, Williams, he introduced himself by saying, "I know more of your songs than *you* do."

● ● ●

Did Kurt Cobain really write all the songs on Hole's *Live Through This?*

Well, the only people who know for sure are Kurt Cobain and Courtney Love. Cobain's dead, and if that rumor were true, it'd be surprising if Love let on now.

Here are the basic arguments from those who think he wrote the album. (1) Courtney Love never made an album anywhere as good as *Live Through This,* either before or after. (2) It would be in character for both of them: Cobain would enjoy turning Love loose on the world with an arsenal of kick-ass songs, and Love wouldn't be above accepting them. (3) In 1996, a widely circulated bootleg emerged of Cobain singing the Hole song "Asking for It," and stories circulated of there being tapes of Cobain singing most of the Hole record. Love's camp floated the story that the intention had been to release a version of Cobain and Love singing the song together, as a treat for

fans who craved the notion of grunge's first
couple duetting like Barbra Streisand and Neil
Diamond doing "You Don't Bring Me Flowers."
(4) One Hole track, "Old Age," an outtake from the
Live Through This sessions, appeared abroad in
1993 as the B-side to "Beautiful Son," with
Courtney Love listed as sole songwriter. In 1998,
however, a boombox tape surfaced of Nirvana
rehearsing "Old Age" in 1991, with some differences but still recognizably the same song; bassist
Krist Novoselic confirmed that the song had been
written by Cobain.

Here are the basic arguments of those who
think he didn't write it. (1) Isn't it a bit sexist to
assume that when a great female rock star
emerges, her success is actually because of a
man? (2) The songs on *Live Through This* don't
really sound like anything else Kurt Cobain
ever did.

Here's some more information: When I interviewed Cobain at his Seattle home in the summer
of 1993, he said that he loved playing music with
Love, and found it rejuvenating, but that they
probably wouldn't ever release any of their
collaborations because it was a bit too redolent of
John and Yoko. He did say that they had written
"Pennyroyal Tea" together. (By other people's
accounts, though, the song was written years

before Cobain met Love.) In October 1993, Cobain visited the Atlanta studio where Hole was recording *Live Through This.* While he was there, Love dragooned him into singing background vocals on a few songs; according to the producers of *Live Through This,* Cobain seemed completely unfamiliar with the songs (which included "Asking for It"). That day was the source of the tape that later leaked; why a ludicrous story about a duet for the fans seemed preferable remains a mystery. Although his vocals are mixed very low on the final version of *Live Through This,* Cobain is audible in spots.

Here's my theory, which you may choose not to believe, but which has the advantage of conforming to the facts as we know them: Courtney Love is a talented lyricist and songwriter who can't quite put the pieces together. She has a gift for turning a sharp phrase, she has good taste in music, and she can come up with a good hook— but for some reason, she doesn't have the ability (focus? patience?) to assemble a full song. What she really needs is an editor to make her ideas work, just as Stevie Nicks has said she needed Lindsey Buckingham to shape her raw musical material. ("He could take my songs and do what I would do if I had his musical talent," Nicks said [in an interview conducted by Love!]. "When he wasn't angry with me, that is. That's why there's seven or eight great songs, and there's fifty more where he wasn't happy with me and didn't help me.") Cobain was an excellent editor, which is why *Live Through This* is Love's best work. In addition, Love was something of a magpie; there are anecdotes about Cobain working on a riff at home, seeing Love get interested, and telling her, essentially, "Hands off that one." I think that Cobain gave her permission to rework "Old Age" and helped improve her songs in various other ways, but that the songwriting on *Live Through This* is essentially hers.

If Cobain polished Love's raw songs, it would be perfectly reasonable to think of his role as editorial. Some people, however, would define the work he did as collaborative. And that's why after he died, some of Love's attempts to draft other people to take his place have ended up messily; for example, after Billy Corgan helped Love with some of the songs on *Celebrity Skin,* they had a public argument over how much credit he deserved. Corgan called his role on the album "Svengali";

> Reliable sources say that despite all his rage, Billy Corgan is still just a rat in a cage. For the details of his fracas with Pavement, see p. 110 in Chapter 8.

Love preferred "music teacher." She recently semi-coherently summed it up like this: "*Live Through This* is formless, has no information except these chords I learned from Billy and certain things I learned from Kurt—[take] really boring three chords and make them fucking magical."

• • •

Is Bachman-Turner

Overdrive's "You Ain't Seen Nothin' Yet" about herpes?

Well, with lyrics such as "She took me to her doctor and he told me of a cure," you might think so. Here's the problem: "The song's from the early 1970s. Herpes wasn't even around then," Randy Bachman said to me, genuinely flabbergasted by the question. (Actually, herpes has been around for millennia—the Roman emperor Tiberius outlawed kissing because of it—but it didn't become epidemic again until the early '80s.) The song was never intended for release; Bachman used it to test the audio levels in the studio and made up the lyrics off the top of his head. The famous stuttering was done to tease his brother Gary, who suffered from a speech impediment; Bachman intended to press just one copy of the song and give it to Gary. Over his objections, the record company released it as a BTO single instead, and it hit number one around the world in 1974. "Then Gary stopped stuttering," Bachman told me.

● ● ●

The White Stripes—what's the deal with those two crazy kids? Brother and sister? Boyfriend and girlfriend?

Neither: Jack White and Meg White were married from September 12, 1996, to March 24, 2000. (Jack took Meg's last name—he was originally Gillis.) The band started while they were still married; their divorce came the same year they released their second album, *De Stijl.*

There're all sorts of jokes we could make here, but they all inevitably spiral into smarmy insinuations about Jack White sleeping with his sister, so let's be content with the facts: They are ex-husband and -wife.

Want to know more about the White Stripes song "Hotel Yorba"? Your reservation has been made, and a mint awaits you on your pillow, on p. 137 of Chapter 10.

● ● ●

I heard that one member of ABBA came from a Nazi family—is that true?

The father of Anni-Frid Lyngstad (aka "the brunette girl") was a Nazi soldier—but she never knew him. In 1943, German sergeant Alfred Haase arrived in Ballangen, Norway. He was twenty-three years old, had a wife at home, and was part of a despised occupying army, but he successfully wooed local girl Synni Lyngstad with a bag of potatoes. (She reciprocated with whale meat.) Their last night together left Lyngstad pregnant with Anni-Frid, born in 1945. Synni Lyngstad's mother knew that because the child was a *tyskerunge*—the illegitimate child of a German soldier—she would be ostracized. So she relocated with her granddaughter to Sweden, where twenty-eight years later, ABBA formed. The Lyngstad family believed that Haase's ship home had been sunk, but in 1977, he turned up in West Germany, convinced ABBA's management that he wasn't a fraud, and met his superstar daughter.

● ● ●

Have any twins been in rock bands before Good Charlotte?

Joel and Benji Madden have a lot more company than you think—and we're not even counting the Cocteau Twins or the Glimmer Twins. Fill your eyes with this double vision: Kim and Kelley Deal of the Breeders, Matthew and Gunnar Nelson of the '90s pop-metal band Nelson, recent pop duo Evan and Jaron (last name Lowenstein), Herbert and Harold Kalin of the '50s harmony duo the Kalin Twins, Craig and Charlie Reid of the Scottish pop-folk Proclaimers, Jay and Michael Aston of the '80s goth band Gene Loves Jezebel, Claude and Cliff Trenier of the '50s jump-blues group the Treniers, and Maurice and Robin Gibb of the Bee Gees. (Often assumed to be twins, but separated by almost three years, are the albino brothers Johnny and Edgar Winter.) In addition, Alanis Morissette has a twin brother, while both Elvis Presley and Justin Timberlake had twin siblings who died at birth.

● ● ●

Is it true that Jim Gordon, drummer on practically every '70s album, is in prison for killing his mother?

Gordon was a top session drummer from 1963 to 1973, keeping time for John Lennon, George

Harrison, Frank Zappa, Traffic, Steely Dan, and Derek and the Dominoes. (He also wrote the elegant piano part that became the second half of "Layla.") But tragically, he spent the '70s wrestling with schizophrenia. "The voices were chasing me around," Gordon said in 1985. "Making me drive to different places. Starving me. I was only allowed one bite of food a meal. And if I disobeyed, the voices would fill me with a rage, like the Hulk gets." He checked himself into psychiatric hospitals at least fourteen times in six years. On June 1, 1983, he checked himself out; two days later, he killed his mother with a hammer and a butcher knife. Gordon was convicted of second-degree murder (California law made it extremely difficult to prove insanity), and remains in prison today.

● ● ●

Are Victoria Williams and Lucinda Williams related?

"I've traced my lineage back to my great-grand-father Captain Williams, who came over from Wales when he couldn't be on the sea anymore," Victoria Williams told me when I called her. "And Lucinda and I aren't related, although you can say we might be. You know, her father's name is Miller and my mother's maiden name is Miller." Neither Lucinda nor Victoria is related to Hank Williams, Vanessa Williams, or Wendy O. Williams.

● ● ●

I heard that *Saved by the Bell*'s Dustin Diamond and the Beastie Boys' Mike Diamond are related—and they do look similar. Is there any truth to this?

So many parallels! In his spare time, Dustin likes a good game of chess; the Beasties while away the hours with Boggle. And Dustin Diamond portrayed Screech on *Saved by the Bell,* while Mike D. and the other Beasties had girlies back at the hotel, and all changed places when they rang the bell. Dustin Diamond has said, "We both have similar features, like our noses. Everyone thinks we're brothers." He added, "Mike Diamond and Dustin Diamond is a coincidence. We both play bass—coincidence." Um, no, that's Adam Yauch on bass; Mike D. plays the drums.

Neither Dustin nor Mike Diamond is related to Neil Diamond; for secret connections to the bard of Brooklyn, turn on your heartlight and see p. 123 in Chapter 9.

• • •

Did Ann and Nancy Wilson of Heart hang out with the Manson Family?

You're probably confusing the Wilson sisters with the Wilson brothers—Brian, Carl, and Dennis— who were the core of the Beach Boys. In 1968, drummer Dennis Wilson picked up two nubile hitchhikers, took them back to his house for an afternoon ménage à trois, and then left for a recording session. When he returned that night, he found they had invited some friends over. His house was filled with naked young hippie girls having a party—and their leader, Charles Manson.

Manson and his acolytes stayed with Wilson for most of the year, spending his money and providing an ongoing orgy. Manson fancied himself a songwriter, so Wilson took him over to Brian's home studio to record some demos—a session that ended when Manson pulled a knife on him. The Beach Boys even recorded one of Manson's songs, "Cease to Exist," renaming it "Never Learn Not to Love" and releasing it as a B-side. When Dennis was asked in 1971 why he didn't give Manson songwriting credit, he replied,

"He didn't want that. He wanted money instead. I gave him about a hundred thousand dollars' worth of stuff." Even before the Manson Family began their killing spree in 1969, Dennis realized they were bad news. He couldn't kick them out of his home without provoking Manson's wrath, so while the Beach Boys were on tour, he found a new place to live and let the lease expire on his old house.

● ● ●

Is Gibby of the Butthole Surfers really the son of a TV children's-show host?

"He wore a red and white striped outfit and a straw hat, and he had a cane, just like the Music Man," remembered lead singer/provocateur Gibby Haynes when we had lunch. His father, Jerry Haynes, was the star of the syndicated *Mr. Peppermint* show, originating on Dallas's WFAA station from 1961 to 1973, and *Peppermint Place* on KERA-TV from 1975 to 1996. The notion of Fred Rogers spawning Damien is entertaining enough that a false rumor long circulated that Frank Zappa was the son of Mr. Greenjeans (from *Captain Kangaroo*). With Gibby, however, who sang scabrous classics such as "Shah Sleeps in

Lee Harvey's Grave," the legend is true: He's actually a former "gumdrop" from Peppermint Place.

The show featured puppets such as Jingles the Dragon, Captain Candy, and Mr. Wiggly Worm (which was basically an overexcited yellow latex glove). As Mr. Peppermint, Jerry Haynes had his own theme song, written by Henry Mancini, and endorsed a line of children's clothes and dog food. On the air, he would do simple science experiments and lead imaginary expeditions to the North Pole. Gibby remembered his dad's on-air cool: Even on days when the scenery was literally collapsing all around him, he could give a smooth intro to the next cartoon. "It was a totally live show in the '60s," Haynes said. "One time he had a rattlesnake shit on his arm on live television. And he had monkeys developing diarrhea mid-cartwheel, like a rooster tail of shit."

In the line of hosting duties, Mr. Peppermint was also attacked by a police dog and told by a young boy that he liked his morning buttermilk with a pinch of bourbon. In 1989, his thoroughly wholesome show was the subject of some unexpected controversy; it was pulled from a Florida station when religious groups complained that some footage of Japan included a picture of a Buddha statue (a graven image) and that the antilittering extraterrestrial Kelli Green character would encourage mysticism. Jerry has also spent time as a cooking-show assistant and on the sports desk, not to mention working as a character actor in movies including *RoboCop, Hard Promises,* and *Boys Don't Cry.*

So how does dad feel about the Butthole Surfers' music, which includes albums such as *Rembrandt Pussyhorse* and *Locust Abortion Technician?* "He's a really cool guy," Gibby reported. "He doesn't like it, but he says he does."

8

DIRTY DEEDS DONE DIRT CHEAP

Fisticuffs, Handcuffs, and Feuds

Noel Gallagher, guitarist and songwriter for Oasis, understood what his job was in a way that seems to come instinctively to British musicians: He was a rock star, and that meant he not only had license to engage in inappropriate behavior, but people would laud him for it. When I interviewed him, as his band started to break through in the United States, he trashed Blur constantly ("They're just pseudo-middle-class Cockney twats, egotistical, confrontational, paranoid wimps"), tried to start a new feud with Pearl Jam any time he got the chance ("I wish Eddie Vedder would get on with it and kill himself"), and told stories about waking up in a Detroit hospital after a seventy-two-hour drug binge. "People encourage rock stars to act like children," he said. "You can act like a big spoiled baby and people think it's great."

• • •

Did a girl really get killed in the studio while the Ohio Players were recording "Love Rollercoaster," and if you listen close you can hear her screams?

If there was *ever* a time to redub a vocal track, you'd think it would be to remove evidence of a homicide, wouldn't you? This story comes in many versions, of which the most lurid is that the naked model getting sticky on the cover of the Ohio Players' 1975 *Honey* was horribly disfigured during the photo shoot because the "honey" was an acrylic substance that bonded with her skin. When she came to the studio demanding justice, the band's manager stabbed her. But the scream—which comes in the breakdown, about two minutes and thirty seconds into the track— is actually keyboardist Billy Beck screeching, like Mariah Carey does en route to a high note. The band believes that the grisly rumors got started by DJs speculating on-air; needless to say, law enforcement has never investigated the fictional murder. "We've never been arrested or incarcerated or interrogated," Ohio Players drummer Jimmy "Diamond" Williams informed me cheerfully. "Some of us have been *handcuffed*—we've had some wild times—but that's different."

• • •

Was there any kind of a feud going on between Steely Dan and the Eagles in the '70s?

In the steel-cage death match of tasteful '70s rock bands lacking muscle tone, Steely Dan fired the first shot, on their 1976 album *The Royal Scam*. "Everything You Did," a bitter, vengeful song directed at a lover, features the line "turn up the Eagles, the neighbors are listening." Glenn Frey of the Eagles said, "Apparently Walter Becker's girlfriend loved the Eagles, and she played them all the time. I think it drove him nuts. So, the story goes that they were having a fight one day and that was the genesis of the line." Given that the two bands shared a manager (Irving Azoff) and that the Eagles proclaimed their admiration for Steely Dan, this was more friendly rivalry than feud. Nevertheless, on "Hotel California" that same year, the Eagles sent a barbed-wire kiss back to Steely Dan with the lyric "They stab it with their steely knives, but they just can't kill the beast." Frey commented, "We just wanted to allude to Steely Dan rather than mentioning them outright, so 'Dan' got changed to 'knives,' which is still, you know, a penile metaphor."

● ● ●

What was the deal with Chuck Berry and those bathroom cameras?

Berry owned the Southern Air restaurant in Wentzville, Missouri, a landmark on Interstate 70—although he was never able to get a liquor license because of his armed-robbery conviction back in 1944. At the end of 1989, Hosana Huck, a cook at the Southern Air, sued the then-sixty-three-year-old Berry, saying that he had made videotapes of her changing clothes in the bathroom and using the toilet. The unwillingly naked chef was soon joined by many others who claimed they had been videotaped, either at the Southern Air or at the rocker's Berry Park estate; sixty women filed a class-action lawsuit against Berry. Although Berry ultimately conceded the hidden-camera tapes existed, he claimed ignorance as to who had made them.

The following year, unsurprisingly, the Southern Air went out of business. At the end of 1994, after the Supreme Court declined to hear Berry's appeal, he quietly settled all the videotape suits for about $1.3 million, putting the lie to his claim in his song "Thirty Days" that if he got no satisfaction from the judge, he would take it to the FBI as a personal grudge.

Legendary producer Phil Spector had some bathroom misadventures of his own; he shares them on p. 173 of Chapter 12.

● ● ●

A friend told me that Son of Sam would pump himself up by listening to Hall & Oates—can that be true?

David Berkowitz's musical tastes aren't well-documented, but Daryl Hall certainly believes his music was on Son of Sam's playlist (competing with the voices in his head). "What I was told is that during the police interrogations with Berkowitz, he said he listened to 'Rich Girl' to motivate himself," Hall said to me in a rapid-fire cadence, referring to the Hall & Oates single, which hit number one during the spring of 1977, when Berkowitz was in the middle of his killing spree. "I don't remember exactly how I heard—maybe one of the detectives." Hall was sufficiently startled by the news that he wrote a song about it, "Diddy Doo Wop (I Hear the Voices)." It included such lyrics as "Charlie liked the Beatles / Sam, he liked 'Rich Girl'," and provided the title for the duo's 1980 album *Voices*. "People interpret things in crazy ways," Hall mused. "Girls come up to me all the time and say, 'I'm a maneater.' And I'm thinking, 'That's *disgusting,* you don't want to tell me *that*.' "

● ● ●

Why were the Kinks banned from playing the United States in the '60s?

Some things went well on the Kinks' first American tour, in the summer of 1965. The group discovered the pleasures of pizza, malted milkshakes, and buxom groupies. But the band was in turmoil; earlier that year, guitarist Dave Davies and drummer Mick Avory had had a fight onstage in Wales, which started with Davies spitting at Avory and ended with Avory hitting Davies over the head with the pedal to his high-hat cymbal. So none of the Kinks were speaking to each other, and on any given night, the band's management wasn't sure how the Kinks would behave—

whether they would do a full show, or come to blows, or treat the audience to a forty-five-minute version of "You Really Got Me" (as the band's road manager says they did one evening, although a roadie insists they didn't play the song for the *entire* show).

While singer Ray Davies has called tales of the Kinks' American misbehavior "character assassination, [a] plot to destroy us," sources close to the band confirm that they found trouble wherever they went, at least some of it of their own making. The band skipped a show in Sacramento, Ray Davies punched a union official who kept insinuating that England was already as good as Communist, and they appeared on a Dick Clark special for NBC without paying their mandatory dues to the American Federation of Television and Radio Artists. The upshot was that the federation blacklisted them—although they never gave a specific reason as to why—and the Kinks could not return to the States for over four years. Years later, Ray Davies mused, "In many respects, that ridiculous ban took away the best years of the Kinks' career, when the original band was performing at its peak."

● ● ●

Did George Harrison bet Jimmy Page that he couldn't write a ballad?

Not really—but he practically dared him to write one. When Harrison met Led Zeppelin drummer John Bonham, the Beatle told him, "The problem with your band is that you don't do any ballads." Of course, this ignores a glorious history of Zeppelin ballads on their first four records, which by 1973 included "Tangerine," "Going to California," and even "Thank You," which dates all the way back to *Led Zeppelin II,* in 1969. Nevertheless, Page took the comment as a spur and wrote "The Rain Song," which was included on Zeppelin's fifth album, *Houses of the Holy.* If you listen carefully to the intro, there's a subtle but unmissable musical tribute to Harrison. Page has explained, "I purposely stuck the first two notes of 'Something' on 'The Rain Song.' "

> The Beatles and Led Zeppelin crossed over in another way: they were both guests at Seattle's famous Edgewater Inn, although Zep got into a lot more trouble there, as detailed on p. 69 of Chapter 5.

● ● ●

Did Jim Morrison really whip it out in Florida?

On March 1, 1969, when the Doors played the Dinner Key Auditorium in Miami, Morrison showed up late, drunk, and in the mood to experiment with confrontational theater. In an antagonistic monologue, he told the crowd, "Your faces are being pressed into the shit of the world," and later doffed his shirt and asked, "Do you want to see my cock?" Some eyewitnesses swore that he then flashed the audience; others insist that he tugged at his pants but never actually revealed his lizard. Organist Ray Manzarek (presumably an expert on the Doors' organs) said Morrison was using the shirt as a matador's cape in front of his crotch, and it was impossible to tell: "I don't know if he pulled it out . . . I think he hypnotized everybody." In a trial the following year, Morrison testified that he kept it in his pants, and had even been wearing boxer shorts that night: "It was kind of unusual, really, because I don't usually wear undergarments. I got out of the habit four or five years ago." Morrison was found guilty of

Read all about Jim Morrison's torrid affair with chanteuse Nico, with lurid details from Ray Manzarek, on p. 122 of Chapter 9.

indecent exposure and open profanity, both misdemeanors. His sentence (six months of hard labor, plus a $500 fine) was on appeal when he died in 1971.

● ● ●

What was the feud

between Smashing Pumpkins and Pavement? How'd it start?

On Pavement's 1994 album *Crooked Rain, Crooked Rain,* their song "Range Life" included this lyric about touring with the Smashing Pumpkins: "Nature kids, but they don't have no function / I don't understand what they mean and I could really give a fuck." For understandable reasons, Corgan took umbrage. "I think it's rooted in jealousy," he said. "There's always been flak we've gotten from certain bands that somehow we cheated our way to the top." Pavement had never toured with the Pumpkins at the time of the song. They said Corgan took measures to maintain that status, keeping them off the '94 Lollapalooza package (he denied it). "But we got on the next year," noted Pavement guitarist Scott Kannberg. "Sonic Youth, Hole, Beck: a much cooler year." The feud never escalated to gunplay or beatdowns, just Corgan's final insult: "People don't fall in love to Pavement . . . They put on Smashing Pumpkins or Hole or Nirvana, because these bands actually mean something to them."

● ● ●

I heard the army tried to draft Frank Zappa because he was a pornographer—is that right?

Well, Zappa did serve time on a pornography charge when he was twenty-three, but he was never a budding Hefner. In 1964, Zappa was playing with a blues trio in a Latino club in Ontario, California, where the crowd was more interested in the four go-go girls onstage wearing fishnet stockings than in the band. A used-car salesman offered Zappa $100 for a sex audiotape. Zappa enlisted the assistance of one go-go girl, Lorraine Belcher, and "stayed up most of the night manufacturing this bogus sex tape, fake bed-springs, squeaks and grunts. I overdubbed a musical background and spent hours cutting the laughs out of this thing." The next day, the salesman proved to be Sergeant Jim Willis of the San Bernardino County Sheriff's Office, running a sting operation.

Zappa was charged with conspiracy to manu-facture pornographic materials—a felony. He bailed out Belcher with his royalties from "Memories of El Monte," a song he had cowritten for the doo-wop group the Penguins. Too broke to mount an effective defense, Zappa pled nolo contendere and served ten days of a six-month sentence (the rest was suspended). "You can't appreciate what a jail is and what goes on there unless someone sticks you in one," Zappa said. "In a way, I guess I have to thank Detective Willis and the evil machinery of the San Bernardino legal system for giving me a chance to see, from that perspective, what the penal system is like in this country, and . . . how ineffectual and how stupid it is."

For another surprising rock/porn connection, check out the Bee Gees' choice of studios on p. 27 of Chapter 2.

Zappa was also given three years' probation, during which he was not permitted to be in the company of any woman under twenty-one without the presence of a "competent adult." But the charge actually kept him *out* of Vietnam—as a convicted felon, he was exempt from the draft.

● ● ●

A friend told me Gregg Allman shot himself to avoid serving in Vietnam—is that true?

Gregg Allman celebrated his eighteenth birthday in 1965—not a good year for that moment to come if your plans didn't include being drafted by the U.S. Army. His older brother, Duane, was exempt from the draft, being the eldest son in a family without a father; however, Duane was determined that the army wouldn't get his little brother and musical partner. (Their band at that point was called the Allman Joys; the Allman Brothers Band lineup didn't come until 1969.)

Gregg remembered, "My brother said, 'I'll tell you what we're gonna do. Just shoot a bullet through your foot.' I thought he was joking. He wasn't." So the night before Gregg's physical examination, Duane threw him a "foot-shootin' party," plying him with speed and whiskey and inviting over some friends and some girls. Gregg painted a target on his left moccasin. "I didn't want to hurt myself," Gregg said. "The long bones in your foot come to a V, and I wanted to hit it right there so it would crack two of them but not really upset anything permanently."

Faced with the actual act of shooting himself, however, Gregg understandably had second thoughts—but Duane wouldn't let him back down, calling him "chickenshit" and saying, "I invited these nice ladies over here to see a foot-shootin' and you're going to let them down?" So

Gregg slammed down some more whiskey and called an ambulance. As soon as he could hear the sirens, *bang!*—he pulled the trigger. Many musicians shoot themselves in the foot metaphorically, but Gregg pulled off the rare stunt of doing it literally.

"I was bleeding quite a bit because the speed and liquor had my blood pressure going," Gregg said. In the rush to the hospital, he and Duane forgot the target he had painted on the moccasin, so Duane later had to sneak back into the operating room and grab the mangled shoe, lest somebody report the Allmans to the government. The next day, Gregg showed up at the induction center on crutches with a huge bandage; he was quickly disqualified. Like both Bush and Cheney, Gregg Allman had found a way to avoid Vietnam.

9

CLOSE ENCOUNTERS OF THE ROCK KIND

Odd Couples of the Music World

Bands don't normally hang out with their opening acts. There are exceptions, of course, but most of the time, they're content to check out one show early on the tour to see whether the table is being adequately set. Future shows are spent chilling in the dressing room, the land of complimentary deli trays and scarf-festooned lamps.

I did, however, witness an exception to that rule: the early courtship between Gavin Rossdale of Bush and Gwen Stefani of No Doubt. When I was trailing the Bush arena tour back in 1996, the two were just sneaking off to the tour bus together and halfheartedly denying anything was going on (Rossdale hadn't completely broken things off with another girlfriend yet); now they're married. The other members of No Doubt (who I knew slightly, from when they had been the opening act on the Everclear tour) asked me discreetly but seriously if I knew what was going on, since they never saw Stefani anymore. The other members of Bush knew exactly what was happening, and would jokingly change the title of their hit single "Everything Zen" to "Everything Gwen."

● ● ●

I heard that Axl Rose used to hang out with Depeche Mode. True?

Yes—but only for one night. In 1989, at the Hollywood premiere of Depeche Mode's concert film 101, the Guns N' Roses singer introduced himself to the band as a huge fan—and then proved it by reciting the lyrics to their mournful song "Somebody." He then took them to the Cat House, a favorite heavy-metal club. But when Rose left the Mode, he continued his evening at a friend's barbecue in Beverly Hills, where he reportedly shot a pig. A spokesman for Depeche Mode soon announced that "as strict vegetarians, the band were appalled by [Rose's] behavior and do not wish to associate themselves with anyone who goes round shooting pigs for fun."

● ● ●

A friend told me Peter Wolf of the J. Geils Band and director David Lynch were college roommates—can that be true?

It was a pairing stranger than Felix Unger and Oscar Madison, but for the 1964–65 academic year, Wolf and Lynch were roommates at the School of the Museum of Fine Arts in Boston. The housing office wasn't to blame; Wolf had moved to Boston from the Bronx without a place to live, and spent his first week in town sleeping in a flophouse hotel and at the YMCA. On the first day of school, Lynch spotted him looking at ROOMMATES WANTED notices on a school bulletin board and invited him to share his small apartment. The furniture was provided by Lynch, which meant that they slept in bunk beds: Wolf on the top, Lynch on the bottom.

"I drove David crazy two ways," Wolf told me. "I was always late with the rent, and I was very into progressive jazz at the time—I never stopped playing Thelonious Monk." Both were studying painting, but Wolf was a devotee of German expressionism, while Lynch subscribed to abstract expressionism, so they had heated arguments about the two approaches. Wolf remembered the director of *Eraserhead* and *Mulholland Drive:* "David was a very mellow, very kind guy. But the days we spent together, we were all in a deep shadow of gloom. It was a very nihilistic period. And there were a lot of cockroaches."

● ● ●

Is Sheryl Crow's "My Favorite Mistake" about her relationship with Eric Clapton?

One advantage to being a platinum recording artist is that after a breakup, you can write a bitter kiss-off song and your ex will have to change stations when it comes on the radio. And Crow's had no shortage of celebrity boyfriends who might want to lunge for the dial, including Clapton, Jakob Dylan, Kid Rock, Owen Wilson, and Lance Armstrong. But Clapton can rest easy, according to Crow: "'My Favorite Mistake' is about several people in my life who weren't very good ideas—but not Eric. I've known Eric for over ten

For the full story on "You're So Vain," fly your Lear Jet up to Nova Scotia and turn to p. 145 of Chapter 10.

years, and I can't look at that relationship as a mistake." Crow has also learned from the decades-long intrigue surrounding the inspiration for Carly Simon's "You're So Vain." Crow's declared that when asked who her song's really about, she's "gonna say Warren Beatty or Mick Jagger."

● ● ●

How did Eminem and Dr. Dre meet?

That encounter is as shrouded in mythology as the first meeting between Batman and Robin. Some even claim that Dr. Dre found a copy of *The Slim Shady EP* on the floor of the gym belonging to Jimmy Iovine (president of Interscope Records). In fact, in 1997, Eminem appeared on the syndicated radio program *The Wake Up Show,* where he did some freestyling, which Dre heard and remembered. But Dre wasn't motivated to do anything until Iovine gave him a tape of *The Slim Shady EP.* "In my entire career in the music industry, I've never found anything from a demo tape," Dre said. "When I heard it, I didn't even know he was white."

Dre wanted to meet this unknown talent right away, so Eminem's managers scraped together some money to fly him out to Los Angeles. When he met Dre, a nervous Eminem couldn't even look him in the eye—which made Dre think that Em didn't like his music. "I told him later that I've been a fan of his since I was little, since N.W.A," Eminem said. "I was like, 'Dog, you're mother-fuckin' Dr. Dre!'" The dynamic duo quickly went into the Batcave Studio, where they promptly put together four songs in six hours, including "Role Model" and "My Name Is."

> Extending the Bat-metaphor would make D12 the Justice League of America; more details on p. 77 of Chapter 6.

● ● ●

Did Don Henley and Stevie Nicks have an affair in the '70s?

"He was really cute and he was elegant," Nicks has said of Henley. (Not to cast aspersions on her judgment, but did she look at his hair? Henley sported a 'fro in the '70s that seemed to make up 70 percent of his body weight.) So after Nicks and her Fleetwood Mac bandmate Lindsey Buckingham broke up, circa 1976, she and Henley began an affair. As Nicks remembered it, "This is not popular. Sure, Lindsey and I are totally broken up, I have every right in the world to go out with people, but I spend most of my time with the band, and it's not real conducive to having a relationship." So although Nicks and Henley would later pledge "lovers forever, face to face" on the 1981 hit duet "Leather and Lace," the on-and-off affair lasted only about two years, and they did not found a California rock dynasty.

As for Henley, he's said, "I believe, to the best of my knowledge, [that Nicks] became pregnant by me. And she named the [unborn] kid Sara, and she had an abortion—and then wrote the song of the same name [on Fleetwood Mac's *Tusk*] to the spirit of the aborted baby. I was building my house at the time, and there's a line in the song that says, 'And when you build your house, call me.' "

● ● ●

I heard Prince and Bob Marley recorded a song together. Was it ever released?

Marley's manager, Don Taylor, tried to arrange a collaboration between the two legends in 1979, but he was unsuccessful in his efforts, largely because of Prince's wardrobe, or lack thereof. After a Prince show in Los Angeles, the reggae giant visited him backstage. Taylor said, "When we called on Prince, he met us in this skimpy leopard G-string undergarment, which

Madonna, no stranger to skimpy undergarments herself, was more receptive to working with Prince; see p. 164 of Chapter 12.

immediately aroused Bob's Jamaican macho feelings, and so our stay was as brief as Prince's G-string, and Bob's discomfort was shown all over his face."

● ● ●

I've wondered ever since I saw Oliver Stone's Doors movie—was Nico really Jim Morrison's lover?

Nico and Morrison did have a brief, intense romance circa 1967. Their courtship involved lots of arguing and hair-pulling; Stone focused on blow jobs. (Doors keyboardist Ray Manzarek lauded Nico's oral technique on Morrison at [creepy] length in his autobiography, saying she understood "the proper use of the tongue on the underside of the penis.") Nico (1938–1988), a German-born model and chanteuse, had a long list of liaisons with other rock stars, including Lou Reed of the Velvet Underground (she sang on the group's first record). She said she liked to make pancakes for Reed; John Cale described their affair as "consummated and constipated." After Nico left the Velvets, she had an affair with a teenaged Jackson Browne, who played in her band and wrote "These Days" for her. Her other lovers included Iggy Pop; when the Stooges were getting started, she moved to Ann Arbor and spent three months living with him. ("Nico would try to cook for us," Pop later said, "but she would cook a pot of brown rice and pour half a container of Tabasco sauce in it.") She gave Pop expensive bottles of wine, lessons on how to deal with record-company executives, and, as a bonus, his first case of VD.

> Iggy Pop also had a liaison with model Bebe Buell; she said, "Iggy was a fling with feelings, and it could have been more if he hadn't been on drugs." See p. 33 in Chapter 2 for more on Buell's love connections.

● ● ●

Did the Darkness have to pay Neil Diamond royalty fees for using his line "touching you, touching me"?

It wouldn't be a Darkness lyric if singer Justin Hawkins didn't deliver it in an overdramatic falsetto: You can find the line in their song "I Believe in a Thing Called Love." (*Touching Me, Touching You* was Neil Diamond's breakthrough fifth album.) You can't copyright titles, and it

wasn't a sufficiently distinct lift, so the metallists
didn't have to contribute to Diamond's royalty
statements. "I didn't realize what I'd done until
after," Hawkins informed me. "It was subliminal.
It's astonishing when you look back, at how many
of the all-time great songs he's written—he does
influence everyone's songwriting." An even more
obvious Darkness tribute to Diamond is their track
"Love on the Rocks with No Ice," referring to
Diamond's number two hit ballad from 1980,
"Love on the Rocks."

"I like the way he's so sincere it hurts,"
Hawkins said. "And I love the way that when he's
struggling with a high note, something too painful
for him to reach, he has a whole bunch of backing
singers back him up on it." There have been press
reports that the Darkness and Diamond plan to
write a song together—inevitably a historic
collaboration—but Hawkins said that although he
would love to, they haven't contacted each other
and he doesn't even know if Diamond is aware
that the Darkness exists. So what do Diamond and
Hawkins have in common? "Reveling in the idea
of being miserable," Hawkins said. "And receding
hairlines."

10

I WRITE
THE SONGS

And Then People Wonder
What the Hell I Was Thinking

My lifetime total of songs written stands, at press time, at one. It would probably be zero, except for one fateful assignment: To demonstrate how easy it is for anybody to use ProTools software, *Rolling Stone* sent me to Los Angeles to record a song in the home studio of Butch Vig (drummer for Garbage and producer of Nirvana's *Nevermind*). The fact that I am almost completely devoid of musical talent was regarded as a bonus.

A decade of reading reader-submitted misheard

lyrics for my *'Scuse Me While I Kiss This Guy* books and page-a-day calendars had taught me that most mis-heard lyrics were about either sex or food. Makes sense: they're both primal motivators. But while the pop charts are full of songs about sex and lust, tunes about food are few and far between. I decided to fill the gap and provide the public with what they wanted to hear about, so I called my song "I'm Hungry." The lyrics, mostly written while I was stuck in traffic on the 405 on the way to my hotel, featured such lines as "You want to love me, I don't care / I just want clam sauce on angel hair" and "Grill the vegetables, indirect heat / Set the table, it's time to eat!" After an evening at the house of Butch Vig (who, I should emphasize, exercised superhuman patience with my rank-amateur self) I had decided that writing a song was not, in fact, that hard, and that recording the music was downright easy, especially with a first-class producer doing most of the work. But singing it? For years, I had mocked Billie Joe Armstrong of Green Day, a California boy through and through, for singing with a British accent. To my horror, I found that I did the very same thing myself.

● ● ●

What is Elton John's "Tiny Dancer"
about? My friend says it's some kind of woman-muse, but I think he's singing to his penis.

"That's great!" said a laughing Bernie Taupin, the song's lyricist, when I reached him on the phone. "But I wouldn't belittle myself so." Your friend is closer to the truth, although Taupin emphasized that the song wasn't about any one woman (particularly not his ex-wife, to whom the song is dedicated on *Madman Across the Water*). "We came to California in the fall of 1970, and sunshine radiated from the populace," he said. "I was trying to capture the spirit of that time, encapsulated by the women we met—especially at the clothes stores up and down the Strip in L.A. They were free spirits, sexy in hip-huggers and lacy blouses, and very ethereal, the way they moved. So different from what I'd been used to in England. And they all wanted to sew patches on your jeans. They'd mother you and sleep with you—it was the perfect oedipal complex." Why "tiny," then? "Well, that's poetic license, although they were all petite and lithe. And 'Tiny Dancer' sounds better than 'Small Dancer,' or 'Little Dancer.' "

Another Elton John lyrical mystery comes up later in this chapter; if you can't wait, turn to p. 143.

Does Led Zeppelin's "Ramble On" refer to *The Lord of the Rings,* or am I crazy?

You're not crazy. "'Twas in the darkest depths of Mordor I met a girl so fair / But Gollum, the evil one, crept up and slipped away with her," Robert Plant sings in "Ramble On." This doesn't actually make much sense in terms of the book—Mordor's the last place you'd expect to pick up a girl so fair, and Gollum didn't care for anything except his Precious—but Plant was freely adapting the trilogy for his own song about life on the road. Plant was enough of a J.R.R. Tolkien fan to name one of his dogs "Strider," a name used by Aragorn in the books (and Viggo Mortensen in the movies). In concert, Plant would even shout out "Strider!" during performances of "Bron-Y-Aur Stomp." He also dropped other Tolkien references into his lyrics: The title of "Misty Mountain Hop" refers to Middle Earth geography, while "The Battle of Evermore" mentions "ringwraiths." But that doesn't mean that every Zeppelin song with Celtic or Druidic overtones was a Tolkien pastiche; Plant was a devotee of British mythology and history. Or, as Zeppelin bassist John Paul Jones put it, "Robert was into all that fairy stuff."

• • •

I've never been able to make out the beginning of the second verse in Van Halen's "Everybody Wants Some!!" and there's no lyric sheet. "I tickle mobile line looking for mookie"? Help!

To the best of David Lee Roth's recollection, he intended to sing, "I've seen a lot of people just lookin' for a moonbeam." If you think what he recorded doesn't really sound like that, you're right—by his own admission, sometimes he would forget the words in the studio and "mush-mouth it," approximating syllables. "Sometimes it was attitude, which revved up so hard that it just defies lyrics," Roth said. "There are certain things that shouldn't have too much meaning, like Saturday night." So his best approximation of what came out of his mouth? "Sheepa latta peppah dabba looka foh a moonbeam."

● ● ●

What are the lyrics to Interpol's song "PDA"? No one seems to know.

Interpol vocalist Paul Banks feels your pain. "I've always been the kind of listener who obsesses over lyrics," he told me. "I could give you every 50 Cent lyric. It's not a point of pride;

it's a compulsion." Because of the time Banks spends deciphering other bands' lyrics, and because of his feeling that many great songs are enigmatic, Interpol's albums don't include lyric sheets. Nevertheless, he recently gave in and posted the lyrics on the band's website (www.interpolny.com) out of sympathy for the band's European fans, who are wrestling with English as a second language. The lovely, droning "PDA" is about a breakup (although Banks emphasized that songs he sings in the first person are not necessarily about himself). The chorus is "Sleep tight, grim rite, we have two hundred couches where you can sleep tonight." The word *rite* trips up many people; Banks drily observed, "Homonyms are fun."

● ● ●

How many of the United States has Bruce Springsteen mentioned on his albums?

Sure, sometimes it feels like Springsteen writes his lyrics with a Rand-McNally atlas open at his side. But when you tote up the states he mentions by name (which means that we don't count Tennessee because of a Memphis reference, or "all the northeast state" in "Racing in the Street"), there are only eighteen of them. His home states of New Jersey and California are in the most songs—seven each. The list, for would-be road-trippers: Arkansas, California, Colorado, Florida, Maryland, Michigan, Nebraska, New Jersey, New Mexico, New York, Ohio, Oklahoma, Pennsylvania, Texas, Utah, Virginia, Wisconsin, and Wyoming. If you're a resident of another state and you want Bruce to rectify this slap in the face, we suggest you circulate a petition.

Zoom in on a New Jersey map to find out exactly where E Street was; turn to p. 178 in Chapter 13.

● ● ●

What's that "gizzer"
chorus in Missy Elliott's "Gossip Folks"?

If you thought Snoop Dogg invented the idea of dropping Zs into the middle of words, you've got some catching up to do. The "Gossip Folks" chorus is sampled from Frankie Smith's single "Double Dutch Bus," a number one R&B hit in 1981. Smith, formerly a songwriter with Gamble and Huff's Philadelphia International Records, combined a funk groove, a rap about a bus, and some neighborhood kids doing call-and-response slang flavored with pig Latin. So "It's alrizzight!

Nizzow wizzee wizzill silzzee!" un-Z-ified would be "It's alright! Now we will see!"

• • •

What house, exactly, were Crosby, Stills, and Nash singing about in "Our House"?

It was the house Graham Nash shared with Joni Mitchell in Los Angeles. The most famous facts about that house: (1) It was a very, very fine house, (2) with two cats in the yard. But "Our House," the Crosby, Stills & Nash song that recorded those details, left out some salient information: (3) The house was on Lookout Mountain Road, in the Laurel Canyon neighborhood of the Hollywood hills, epicenter of California's laid-back late-'60s folk-rock scene, and (4) the living room was the location where Nash sang for the very first time with David Crosby and Stephen Stills.

Van Dyke Parks, songwriter and Beach Boys associate, called Laurel Canyon "the seat of the beat." In the summer of 1968, that beat was mellow, tuneful, and full of songs about relationships. The Laurel Canyon population included Carole King, who had relocated after her divorce from Gerry Goffin. Cass Elliot, of the Mamas & the Papas, was hosting Judy Collins, who was rehearsing her band by the pool. Peter Tork had quit the Monkees and was hosting a party that stopped only when his money ran out. And visitor Eric Clapton was carrying around an advance copy of the Band's *Music from Big Pink,* making everyone he met listen to it.

Joni Mitchell, who would perfect the poetry of acoustic heartbreak on albums like *Blue,* and then later bend it into strange new jazzy shapes, was recording her first album. Graham Nash, who had not quite left the Hollies yet, was staying at her house on Lookout Mountain Road. David Crosby, an ex-boyfriend of Mitchell's who had recently been thrown out of the Byrds, was working on some songs with Stephen Stills, of the recently disbanded Buffalo Springfield. (Neil Young, at loose ends after the Springfield's demise, would join Crosby, Stills, and Nash for their second record.) Nash told me, "Me and David's contention and memory, which obviously was affected by various substances which shall remain nameless, marijuana, was that the first time we sang was in Joni's and my living room. Stephen's got a whole different story—he thinks it was Mama Cass's kitchen."

Following the majority, then: The living room had a wooden floor, slightly polished, and a brick fireplace. In front of one large window was an array of small shelves, which held pieces of colored glass, creating a stained-glass effect. In the early evening, Crosby and Stills played one of the songs they had been working on together, "You Don't Have to Cry," with two-part harmony, while Nash and Mitchell listened.

Reaching the end of the song, they asked Nash what he thought. "Play it one more time," he told them. They shrugged and obliged him. When they finished, again he said, "Do me a favor—just play it one more time." And this time, when they sang, he added his high harmony part.

"It became very clear what I was going to be doing for the next twenty years," Crosby said to me. "I tell everyone I'm the best harmony singer in the world—but I'm not, he [Nash] is."

● ● ●

Where did the idea of a prostitute come from in Donna Summer's "Bad Girls"?

Summer hit number one with the disco single "Bad Girls" in 1979—but she says she almost didn't record it. Neil Bogart, head of her record label, Casablanca, originally wanted to give it to Cher. As for the inspiration? "I was in my office in the old Casablanca building," Summer told me. "I was the only artist allowed to have an office there—Neil didn't want me too far away. I sent out my secretary to do something, and the police stopped her on Sunset Boulevard. She was dressed in business attire, but they were trying to pick her up. That ticked me off. All day, I pondered why that would happen to innocent people—and then I developed compassion for the girls working on the street." And the "toot-toot, beep-beep"

> You think that was licentious? How about that extended orgasm Donna Summer had on wax for "Love to Love You Baby"? See p. 163 in Chapter 12.

that punctuated the track? "I figured, what do guys do when they pick up girls? I had to emulate them tooting their horns."

● ● ●

Is the person being addressed in "Hackensack" by Fountains of Wayne ("I see you talkin' to Christopher Walken") real or fictional?

The ballad on the *Welcome Interstate Managers* album is about a high-school crush who's gone on to larger fame ("We sat together in Period One / Fridays at 8:15"). "It's like an updated version of 'Centerfold,' a clean version," said Adam Schlesinger of the Fountains. "Unfortunately, it's a made-up character. I wasn't thinking of a real actress at the time, but if we ever do a video, I want to get Amanda Peet—she's a friend of a friend and she said she'd do it."

•   •   •

Who was Elizabeth Reed, the woman immortalized so beautifully in the Allman Brothers' song?

Not somebody the Allman Brothers ever met, or even knew anything about—other than that she was dead. Elizabeth Reed Napier, born November 9, 1845, was a Southern belle who went to Macon, Georgia, to attend Wesleyan College; she died in 1935. "In Memory of Elizabeth Reed," originally on the album *Idlewild South,* is a lovely, intricate instrumental by guitarist Dickey Betts, who spent a lot of time sitting and writing in the Macon graveyard, where he saw Elizabeth Reed's name. The song was actually inspired by a living girl—but because she was Boz Scaggs's girlfriend, Betts couldn't use her name. "Some writer once asked me how I wrote the song and Duane [Allman] said, 'Aw, he fucked some girl across the tombstone,' " Betts said. "You can imagine how the girl I wrote it for felt after that."

•   •   •

I noticed U2's "Running to Stand Still" doesn't use the title of the song until the very end—are there other songs that use that same trick?

Absolutely, all of them delivering the small charge that comes from delayed gratification. Check out, for example, Peter Gabriel's "Lead a Normal Life," George Michael's "One More Try," or the Cure's "Just Like Heaven." (Rigorously insisting that the singer not repeat or riff on that final lyric excludes contenders such as Prince's "Ballad of Dorothy Parker.") Unfortunately, none of these songs really lend themselves to Penn and Teller's suggestion of how to behave when you're in a movie theater and a character says the movie's title for the first time: Clap politely.

● ● ●

On the White Stripes' album *White Blood Cells,* there's a song called "Hotel Yorba"—is that a real hotel?

Yes, but even if you're the world's biggest White Stripes fan, you probably don't want to spend the night there. It's a run-down building on 4020 Lafayette Boulevard in southwest Detroit, just a few blocks away from the Greyhound bus station. (The band refers to the same street on their single

"Lafayette Blues.") You can't rent rooms by the night at the Hotel Yorba, but one week will set you back just $65. In the song, Jack White contrasts the desolation of the Hotel Yorba with dreams of a home in the country. "There was a great rumor when I was a kid that the Beatles had stayed there," White has said. "They never did, but I loved that rumor." As rock 'n' roll lodgings go, you'd probably rather stay in Leonard Cohen's Chelsea Hotel or Bono's Million Dollar Hotel. (I recommend, however, not spending the night at the fictional Heartbreak Hotel or the enigmatic Neutral Milk Hotel.)

The Beatles did stay at the Edgewater Inn in Seattle, although Led Zeppelin and Vanilla Fudge had a more memorable visit, as detailed on p. 69 of Chapter 5.

• • •

In the first line of "Chuck E.'s in Love," Rickie Lee Jones sings, "How come he don't come and P.L.P. with me down at the meter no more?" What does "P.L.P." mean?

It stands for "public leaning post," old American slang used when one friend leans on another. (If somebody leaned against you, you might say, "What am I, a public leaning post?") The jazzy, bluesy hit (number four in 1979) was an artifact of the bohemian friendship between Jones, her lover Tom Waits, and Chuck E. Weiss; the trio spent lots of time hanging out at the seedy Tropicana Motel in Los Angeles. Although at the conclusion of the song, Jones sings, "Chuck E.'s in love with the little girl who's singing this song," she says the twist ending was fictional. The person Chuck E. was actually smitten with? A cousin of his in Colorado. Waits took the phone call from Denver, where Weiss reported why he had traveled halfway across the country. Waits hung up and in his gravelly voice gave Jones the phrase that would become the cornerstone of her career: "Chuck E.'s in love!"

● ● ●

What exactly were Paul Simon and Julio doing down by the schoolyard? We only know it was against the law.

That's not completely accurate—we also know that it was what the mama saw. Paul Simon's lyrics contain many mysteries, starting with why he says there must be fifty ways to leave your lover but then enumerates only seven. The most enigmatic, however, is the refrain of the 1972 hit "Me and Julio Down by the Schoolyard," where Simon cheerfully sings, "It was against the law / What the mama saw." Asked to shed some light on this criminal act, Simon said, "I have no idea what it is. Something sexual is what I imagine, but when I say 'something,' I never bothered to figure out what it was. Didn't make any difference to me. I like the line about the radical priest—I think that's funny to have in a song."

• • •

I've been wondering:
Were the songs on Wilco's album *Yankee Hotel Foxtrot* written before or after September 11, 2001? If before, they are eerily prophetic. If after, then they are the subtle emotional expression that inspires me with Wilco.

Although *Yankee Hotel Foxtrot* wasn't released until April 2002, the album was completed in June 2001—getting dropped by your record label is not only insulting, it's time-consuming. But "eerily prophetic" is exactly what those lyrics are, especially "Tall buildings shake, voices escape singing sad sad songs" (on "Jesus, Etc."), "Moving forward through flaming doors" (on "War on War"), and the very title of "Ashes of

American Flags." A week after the attack, songwriter Jeff Tweedy said, "We made a record about America, and now it feels like these personal moments are politicized in a way I couldn't have imagined."

● ● ●

Did Barry Manilow really not write "I Write the Songs?"

Nope! Despite the musical declaration "I am music / And I write the songs," Manilow didn't write "I Write the Songs," which hit number one in 1975. Nor did he write his two other number one singles, "Mandy" and "Looks Like We Made It." "I Write the Songs" was actually penned by Bruce Johnston of the Beach Boys. The song was recorded by the Captain and Tennille and David Cassidy before Manilow got his hands on it, which is some sort of strange '70s light-rock trifecta. Manilow did, however, cowrite at least some of the songs that make the young girls cry, including "Copacabana (At the Copa)," "I Made It Through the Rain," and the State Farm commercial jingle, "Like a Good Neighbor."

● ● ●

Who and what is Audioslave's song "Cochise" about?

Contrary to rumor, Cochise was not one of the Sweathogs on *Welcome Back, Kotter.* He was a charismatic Chiricahua Apache war chief born in 1812. In 1861, he and five other Apaches were wrongly accused by a U.S. Army second lieutenant of abducting a ten-year-old boy from an Arizona ranch. Told that he would be held hostage until the boy was returned, Cochise escaped by cutting through the side of a tent. The army then hung their Apache captives, and Cochise waged guerrilla war against the United States until 1872. (When he died in 1874, Geronimo became chief of the Chiricahua Apaches.) There's no reference to Cochise in the lyrics of the Audioslave song, which were written by Chris Cornell; he told me the hectoring song is "Me yelling at me, looking in the mirror." The title, however, came from guitarist Tom Morello. "At the time we were working on the song, I was reading a couple of biographies of Cochise," Morello said to me. "The name refers to the warpath-like vibe of the music. Cochise declared war on the Southwest—you drop the needle on the track and feel that vibe."

● ● ●

This has always bugged me—
what does the line "paying your H.P. demands forever" in Elton John's "Someone Saved My Life Tonight" mean?

That's not H.P. as in Hewlett-Packard, or as in the British brand of brown sauce. (What is "brown sauce," you ask? Well, it's basically bottled gravy, and English supermarkets have aisles full of the stuff. It's probably safer for you if you don't have any more information than that.) The song is about, among other things, John's relief at not getting trapped in an early marriage and all the domestic drudgery and bills that would have gone along with that. H.P. in this context is short for "hire purchase," the no-longer-common British practice that allows you to rent appliances such as a TV for a weekly fee; after some years of rental, you can buy it for a nominal amount, which people called "buying on the H.P." or, sometimes, "buying on the never-never."

● ● ●

How many Randy Newman songs
have the names of cities in their titles?

Not counting his film soundtracks, nine:
"Baltimore," "Birmingham," "Birmingham

Redux," "Christmas in Capetown," "Dayton, Ohio—1903," "Gainesville," "I Love L.A.," "Miami," and "New Orleans Wins the War."

• • •

I need to know: What lyricist said "Angels had guitars even before they had wings"? Please help.

That would be Jim Steinman, the mad-genius songwriter behind Meat Loaf and coiner of such modern proverbs as "We're living in a powder keg and givin' off sparks." The angels line was in his song "Rock & Roll Dreams Come Through." He released it as a solo single in 1981 (the album was the disappointingly limp *Bad for Good*) and it hit number thirty-two. In 1994, Steinman recorded a new version with Meat Loaf, amping up the melodrama, improving the sax solo, and adding a new verse with the "angels had guitars" line. Meat Loaf's version hit number thirteen, proving either that the "angels had guitars" line was worth exactly nineteen places on the Top 40 or that America prefers pop songs when they're sung by 340-pound guys.

• • •

I've heard a million

different stories—who was Carly Simon actually singing about in "You're So Vain"?

Simon's excellent, sinuous single, which hit number one in 1973, probably marked the peak of her career. As critic Ellen Willis said, it proved rock 'n' roll was so democratic, even a rich person could make a great single. (Simon's father was Richard L. Simon, the cofounder of the publishing house Simon & Schuster.) The song was addressed to a rich, self-involved ex-boyfriend, prone to philandering, placing winning bets at the Saratoga racetrack, and flying Lear Jets up to Nova Scotia. "You're so vain / You probably think this song is about you," Simon sang in the chorus.

So who was Simon holding up a well-polished mirror for? Speculation has centered, reasonably enough, around Simon's real-world ex-boyfriends: Mick Jagger, Warren Beatty, Kris Kristofferson, and Cat Stevens—plus James Taylor, who she married a month before the song hit the airwaves.

Let's start with Mick Jagger, who provided backing vocals on the song. If he was, in fact, the subject of the "You're So Vain," that would either mean that Simon had deviously tricked him into singing on the track or that he was just so

arrogant that he didn't care if everybody knew
how vain he was. Simon says that originally Harry
Nilsson was going to do the backing vocals, but
that when Jagger dropped by the London studio
to say hello and pitch in, Nilsson graciously
stepped out. Asked point-blank in 2001 if it was
about Jagger, Simon said, "Oh, no, no, no."

So maybe it was about the famously vain
Warren Beatty, then? Simon says that Beatty
certainly thought so; after the song came out, he
called Simon and thanked her for writing it about
him. (And arguably, anyone who genuinely
believes the song is about himself is vain enough
that the song *should* be about him.) A *Washington
Post* interviewer asked Simon in 1983, "You had
gone with [Beatty]?" Simon replied, "Hasn't
everybody?" "No," the interviewer replied. "That
only means you haven't met him," Simon said. "At
the time I met him, he was still relatively undis-
covered as a Don Juan. I felt I was one among
thousands at that point—it hadn't reached, you
know, the population of small countries." In 2000,
Simon said, "It's certainly not about Warren."

Simon has also specifically ruled out James
Taylor ("It's definitely not about James"). In an
interview with *Rolling Stone* in 1973, soon after
the song's release, she said, "James suspected
that it might be about him because he's very

vain." Apparently, soon after the song's release, Taylor had the discomfiting experience of taking a jet plane to Nova Scotia; fortunately for him, it wasn't a Lear.

At various points, Simon has suggested that the song was actually inspired by three or four different people. Just as consistently, however, she's talked about a specific person being the subject of the song. She could, of course, be engaging in intentional misdirection, but it seems more likely that one particular ex was the inspiration for the song, and that she then garnished that portrait with aspects of some other past paramours, and maybe invented a few details as well. Despite the contrary claims of the lyrics, there may have never been an apricot scarf.

After thirty years of keeping the gavotter's identity a secret, Simon sold the information in 2003 to the high bidder in a charity auction benefiting Martha's Vineyard Community Services. The winner: Dick Ebersol, the NBC Sports president (and one of the executives behind the launch of *Saturday Night Live*). For $50,000, Simon invited him and nine of his friends over to her house, performed the song, swore them to secrecy, and told them who it was about. (In the ensuing wave of publicity, she gave the coy clues that the subject's name contained the letters

E, A, and R—which would eliminate Cat Stevens and Kris Kristofferson, but not Jagger, Beatty, or Taylor.)

Not sworn to secrecy, apparently, is her husband since 1987, Jim Hart. In 2005, he told a small New York newspaper that "You're So Vain" was not about any well-known name—just an old boyfriend of no particular notoriety. This makes sense on a number of levels: Simon could easily have had a jet-setter boyfriend before her singing career took off, and when she said in 1973, "I can't possibly tell who it's about because it wouldn't be fair," she might have meant that she didn't want to pull a civilian into the spotlight unwillingly. And of course, she's smart enough to know that speculation about Jagger and Beatty is more titillating than the reality. Or, as Simon put it, "I could never really solve it because if I did, then no one would have anything to talk to me about."

11

SEX, DRUGS, AND ROCK 'N' ROLL

But Really, in This Chapter, Just the Drugs

I have a long-standing policy when writing feature articles: If I take drugs with somebody I'm writing about, and if I mention in the article that they were consuming an illegal substance (in practice, that means marijuana), then I have to mention my intake as well. It seems only fair to me: If I took a hit off the joint when it was passed around the room, pretending that I didn't would make me a hypocrite. (And most musicians are gentlemen about sharing—the memorable exception being the rapper Coolio, who sucked down most of a joint in the backseat of a limo and offered it to me only when we pulled up to MTV's studios, in the heart of New York's Times Square. Uh, no thanks, dude, I'll decline to walk through Times Square with a joint in my hand.) I never had any problems with this philosophy until I wrote a cover story for *Spin* on Matchbox Twenty and ran up against the magazine's house policy: They deemed it acceptable to write about musicians' drug use, because that's just observational journalism, but forbade writers from writing about their own, because that would be endorsing it. Much tap-dancing ensued; I ultimately wrote a paragraph that implied a great deal without actually depicting anything, not unlike the action of a PG movie.

● ● ●

Did Jimi Hendrix really put LSD on his headband before performing?

The subject of Hendrix and drugs has long been muddled, partly because some members of Hendrix's family insisted that he had never taken any drugs at all, but mostly because the man isn't around to set the record straight himself. (Asked in 1970 if he had "outgrown dope," seven months before his untimely overdose of barbiturates, Hendrix replied, "I don't take as much.") But some fans relish the notion that his technique for taking drugs was as inventive as his guitar playing; a popular rumor has long circulated that he would conceal LSD under his headband and let it enter his body through the pores of his forehead. (The story has variations: Sometimes it's heroin or cocaine that Hendrix had under the headband; sometimes he's supposed to have cut his brow to get the drugs into his bloodstream faster.)

While it's not completely impossible to dose yourself with acid that way—you can get a contact high from handling sheets of blotter acid, and some people have been known to ingest liquid LSD through their eyes—frankly, it would have been a lot of needless effort for Hendrix when he could just have taken the acid orally before going onstage. So you won't find any source on this rumor more reliable than the older brother of some guy you took wood shop with in junior high; Hendrix experts don't lend the story any credence. Jim Fricke, for example, senior curator at the Experience Music Project, the Seattle rock museum with an extensive Hendrix collection, is familiar with the headband rumor, but told me, "I have never heard any backup for that story."

● ● ●

Is Coldplay's song "Yellow" about cocaine?

If the cocaine you've been taking is yellow, it's safe to say that it's not the finest possible grade of Colombian. Originally, "Yellow" had no lyrics at all, except for the word *stars*. When the band was at a studio in Wales, singer Chris Martin came up with the melody while gazing at the night sky, and then sang it for the rest of the band, mimicking the vocal stylings of Neil Young.

When the band returned inside, the word *yellow* caught Martin's eye and the lyrics flowed out of him. "That song is about devotion," Martin has said. "That's just about somebody throwing themselves in front of a car for somebody else." And lyrics about Martin bleeding himself dry, or "Look at the stars / Look how they shine for you"? Martin explained, "You've gotta have overstatement in your songs, haven't you?"

● ● ●

I heard about a drug bust that included Mick Jagger, Keith Richards, and Marianne Faithfull in a fur rug (?) and a chocolate bar (!?!?!), but I don't recall the details. What exactly happened?

It started as a tabloid story: The British paper
News of the World fabricated an article about
Jagger taking drugs in a nightclub. When Jagger
sued for libel, the paper struck back. They found
out that Jagger was visiting Redlands, Richards's
country home in West Wittering, to take LSD (their
source was suspected to be the acid dealer). The
News called the police, who raided Redlands on
February 11, 1967. Jagger, Faithfull, Richards, and
some friends had, in fact, spent the day tripping
on LSD. Faithfull had just taken a bath and
wrapped herself in a fur rug.

The rumor was that Jagger was engaged in
cunnilingus, eating Faithfull and a Mars Bar
simultaneously. "I just sat there in my fur rug,
with no Mars Bar," Faithfull said in 1987. "It's a
folk legend, and if people want to believe that
when the cops walked in there was this incredible
orgy going on, they will, but get it straight." While
Bob Dylan's "Rainy Day Women #12 & 35" played
over and over on the phonograph, the cops
searched those present; Faithfull just dropped her
rug. The police found four benzedrine tablets on
Jagger (which Faithfull says were hers), as well as
a piece of hash, which they returned to him,
thinking it was dirt. At trial, Jagger and Richards
were found guilty and sentenced to three and
twelve months, respectively. On appeal, the

conviction was reduced to probation, and the Glimmer Twins spent only one night in jail, during which Jagger wrote the lyrics for "2000 Light Years from Home."

• • •

What drugs were the Grateful Dead taking when they recorded their first album?

The Dead got their start as the house band at Ken Kesey's acid tests in 1965 and were bankrolled by LSD chemist Owsley Stanley early on, so you'd think the answer would be obvious. But in 1967, while they were recording their album *The Grateful Dead,* they chose a different route to mood alteration: diet pills. The band consumed handfuls of Dexamyl, an amphetamine designed to aid in weight loss, and as a result, some of the tracks, like "Beat It Down the Line," are hopped up and manic (not to mention short—a mere three minutes). "That's what's embarrassing about that record," Jerry Garcia said. "The tempo was way too fast. We were all so speedy at the time."

• • •

Were the Beatles really turned on to LSD by their dentist?

He was a dentist, but not *their* dentist; it's not as if the Fab Four went to get their wisdom teeth collectively extracted and walked out with a tab of acid. The Beatles knew the dentist socially, and one evening in 1965, he hosted a dinner party for John Lennon, George Harrison, and their wives. He slipped some LSD into their after-dinner coffee. "It was, at the time, an unrestricted medication," Harrison said. "I'd heard vaguely about it, but I didn't really know what it was, and we didn't know we were taking it." The dentist didn't partake himself, Harrison said: "I'm sure he thought it was an aphrodisiac. I remember his girlfriend had enormous breasts, and I think he thought there was going to be a big gang bang and that he was going to get to shag everybody."

After dinner, as the group traveled around London, the dose hit. When they took an elevator up to a nightclub, they thought the elevator was on fire. "We were all screaming 'AAAAAAARGH!'" Lennon said. "It was just a little red light." After some misadventures, including Pattie Boyd Harrison attempting to smash a store window, George Harrison took everyone home in his Mini, driving about ten miles per hour.

Reflecting later, Harrison said, "I presumed, mistakenly, that everybody who took LSD was a most illuminated being. And then I started finding that there were people who were just as stupid as they'd been before, or people who hadn't really got any enlightenment except a lot of colors and lights and an *Alice in Wonderland* type of experience. The thing is, after you've had it a couple of times there doesn't seem to be any point to taking it again . . . to change consciousness with a chemical obviously isn't a path to self-realization."

> In 1965, the Beatles also recorded "Norwegian Wood (This Bird Has Flown)." What the hell is Norwegian Wood, anyway? See p. 47 in Chapter 3.

● ● ●

What's the deal with the connections between *The Wizard of the Oz* and *Dark Side of the Moon*? I've seen it, and the connections seem too many to be coincidental. And, I might add, I was neither drunk nor high at the time.

Congratulations on your sobriety: You may be the only person to try this experiment who was not under the influence. In case you haven't heard, here's the deal: If you start playing Pink Floyd's *Dark Side of the Moon* alongside the MGM lion at the beginning of *The Wizard of Oz,* there are

supposed to be some amazing parallels, suggesting that Pink Floyd were deliberately constructing
an alternate score to the movie (or to its first forty-
five minutes, anyway).

In the spirit of scientific experimentation, I tried
it out. (I had a bad head cold, so my inebriant of
choice was NyQuil.) The coolest part is that
"Great Gig in the Sky," the wordless piece with
wailing soul vocals from Clare Torry, plays during
the tornado section, and ends at approximately
the same time as Dorothy's house lands in Oz.
There are some other synchronicities: the alarm
bells start ringing when the villainous Miss Gulch
first appears on-screen; Dorothy balances on the
beam near the pigpen during the lyric "balanced
on the biggest wave"; Glinda shows up while
Roger Waters sings "don't give me that goody-
good bullshit"; and the album-ending heartbeat
sound comes while Dorothy and the Scarecrow
inspect the chest of the Tin Man. Periodically,
people appear to be moving in sync with the
music. Other purported connections seem like
bigger stretches; for example, the Scarecrow does
a crazy dance during the lyric "the lunatic is on
the grass," only he has clearly moved off the grass
and is prancing about on the Yellow Brick Road.

That sounds like a cool list, but the actual
experience is underwhelming. There are long

stretches where the action and the music seem completely disconnected, and the lyrics don't reflect anything happening on-screen, no matter how one stretches. I tried another experiment, playing the Beatles' *Abbey Road* while watching *Pulp Fiction.* Again, there are odd parallels. The opening track, "Come Together," seems to perfectly describe Tim Roth's character: "He just got to be a joker, he do what he please." As the two killers played by John Travolta and Samuel L. Jackson banter, "Maxwell's Silver Hammer" jovially describes another upbeat murderer. John Lennon sings "I want you so bad" just as the title card for "Vincent Vega & Marcellus Wallace's Wife" comes up on-screen, expressing Travolta's uncomfortable lust. "Because the wind is high" is sung as Travolta prepares to shoot up heroin; the drum solo during "The End" seems perfectly in sync with a heated discussion between Travolta and Uma Thurman. Songs end at about the same time that scenes shift; periodically, people seem to be moving in sync with the music.

The moral of the story is this: If you put words and music over a set of images, the human brain will strive to make connections, and there will be some interesting coincidences. Sometimes, it will sync up so closely, it seems hard to believe that it's accidental—especially if you're stoned. Writer

Rob Sheffield brilliantly tried playing *Dark Side of the Moon* over a variety of movies, and found some synchronicities in all of them. The best was *Goodfellas,* where the ending heartbeat coincided elegantly with the guy inside the car trunk trying to get out.

Keep in mind that nobody seems to have noticed the *Wizard of Oz* "connection" until twenty years after *Dark Side*'s release (in other words, once the movie was widely available on home video and CDs had taken hold). So if the connection was intentional, Pink Floyd would have gone to great efforts to do a half-assed job of creating an alternate score for the film, and then asked everyone who worked on the record to keep it secret for decades (nobody associated with the band has ever said it was deliberate). Guitarist David Gilmour has dismissed the connection, saying it was imagined by "some guy with too much time on his hands."

CHAPTER

12

STUDIO SYSTEM

Life in the Recording Studio

One question that I kept asking musicians for years, even though I don't think I *ever* got a good response: What was the most memorable day in the studio while you were recording the album? Generally, when asked this question, their eyes would glaze over and they would feebly try to dredge up something interesting that happened. Here's the truth: Most of the time, working in the studio is a tedious slog with lots of time spent tuning and miking drums and balancing levels and focusing on the minutiae of

ProTools edits. But the perception of the studio as creative crucible persists, and any good studio has seen its fair share of magic over the years. About a decade ago, I realized just how potent the studio myth is when I went to interview Depeche Mode, who were recording their latest album in London at the legendary Abbey Road studios. At the end of the evening, my taxicab pulled away and I shamelessly gawked at the famous intersection where the Beatles had posed for their album cover. (It looked much the same, except the Beatles weren't there.) As I headed back to my hotel, I realized that while Depeche Mode were nice enough guys, I hadn't been particularly thrilled to meet them. But catching sight of Abbey Road—that was when every ounce of cynicism drained out of me and I became a starstruck teen again.

• • •

What's the deal with that weird German phrase at the beginning of Def Leppard's "Rock of Ages"?

"It's meaningless drivel, basically," Def Leppard lead singer Joe Elliott told me, after we discussed the effectiveness of cabbage-soup diets. The drivel in question—which Elliott spells *Gunter gleben glousen globen*—was uttered by the producer of their *Pyromania* record, Mutt Lange (who would later marry Shania Twain). The band was going stir-crazy in the studio (not realizing that future albums with Lange would take years instead of months to complete) and badly needed some comic relief. So on a skeletal version of the "Rock of Ages" track, when Lange was counting off mid-song to indicate where guitar fills should come in, he started off with the traditional "1, 2, 3, 4," progressed to rhythmically listing Indian foods such as papadum, and ended up making up his own quasi-Teutonic language. "We thought it was so funny, we lifted it from the middle of the song," Elliott said. (The Offspring agreed in 1998, borrowing it for the intro of "Pretty Fly [For a White Guy].") "We were actually accosted by a German once who said it meant 'running through the forest, silently'," Elliott reported. "It doesn't— but *auf wiedersehen*, mate!"

● ● ●

When Donna Summer

recorded "Love to Love You Baby," was she actually having an orgasm while humping the floor?

"Love to Love You Baby," Summer's 1975 American breakthrough, boasts moans of pleasure that would not be equaled until Duran Duran's

"Hungry Like the Wolf." *Time* magazine calcu-
lated that twenty-two different orgasms were
audible in the seventeen-minute mix, produced
by Giorgio Moroder, but Summer insisted that
although she was writhing on the studio floor
while she recorded her vocal, she was faking it. In
addition, she clarified when I
got her on the phone, she
wasn't prone on the studio
floor. "I was on my *back*," she
said. "I couldn't do the song
with four guys staring at me,
so I lay down on the floor; we put up curtains and
shut the lights off."

Toot-toot, beep-
beep: the inside story
on "Bad Girls" is
found on p. 134 of
Chapter 10.

● ● ●

Did Prince play guitar on Madonna's "Act of Contrition"?

Madonna's 1989 album *Like a Prayer,* arguably her
finest full-length record, ends with "Act of
Contrition," which is, well, a novelty track. The
Andrae Crouch Choir from the title track returns,
only now the tape is run backward, and there's a
skronking guitar solo. It's chaotic, and even a little
scary, in an Old Testament-meets-Danceteria way.
Madonna fumbles through a half-forgotten prayer
from her Catholic childhood. "I reserve . . . I

resolve," she says. "I have a reservation. *What do you mean it's not in the computer?*"

That apocalyptic guitar certainly sounds like Prince showing off. He and Madonna collaborated on another track on the same album—the grinding, not really successful "Love Song," which was largely done by the two of them mailing tapes back and forth to each other. But the credits for "Act of Contrition" just say, "Produced by the Powers That Be." Asked about the song's creation, Madonna said she improvised the lyrics: "Whatever was in my head. It's totally unedited." And Prince? "He played guitar on it. He also played guitar on 'Keep It Together,' " which hit number eight in 1990—one more gold single for the Paisley Park walls. "We didn't have to prove anything to each other," Madonna analyzed. "And I don't think he's had that same opportunity with other people that he's worked with. Because generally he tends to dominate everything."

● ● ●

Is it true that Pink Floyd recorded a complete album using only household objects?

No, but they tried. After *Dark Side of the Moon* hit number one in 1973, making Pink Floyd inter-national superstars, the band returned to Abbey

Road studios that fall, not sure what to do next. "What do we do after *this?*" asked keyboardist Rick Wright. Although their record company would probably have preferred *Dark Side II: The Lunatic Returns,* the band set off on a more experimental route.

They decided to record an album without musical instruments, using only common household objects. "If you tap a wine bottle across the top of the neck," guitarist David Gilmour said, "you get a tabla-like sound close up." Pink Floyd explored other sounds: They stretched rubber bands between two tables (for a bass sound), they unrolled adhesive tape at various lengths, they sawed wood, they pounded hammers, they chopped tree trunks with axes, they broke lightbulbs. The band's road manager was sent out to hardware stores to find brooms with a wide variety of bristle strengths.

As the weeks went by, it became apparent that while the band was enjoying their mad-scientist recording experiments, not much progress was being made, and the sounds were not an improvement on using traditional instruments such as guitars and drums. Engineer Alan Parsons remembered, "We spent something like four weeks in the studio and came away with no more than one and a half minutes of music."

Only one fragment of the work would ever appear on a Pink Floyd record. Their next album, 1975's *Wish You Were Here,* features one of the sounds on the introduction to the first epic track, "Shine on You Crazy Diamond." Drummer Nick Mason said, "We had used an old party trick of filling wineglasses with varying levels of water and then running a finger round the rim to create a singing tone. These tones were then put onto sixteen-track tape and mixed down in chord clusters so that each fader controlled an individual chord." As it turns out, the band had created a high-tech reinvention of an old musical instrument, one that Benjamin Franklin had also designed a version of: the glass harmonica.

● ● ●

I think the bassline for Chic's "Good Times" is the greatest bass part ever recorded. Where did it come from?

One of the pleasures of listening to old Chic records is the virtuosity of each of the three musicians in the band; you can focus on any one part all the way through a song and marvel at the playing. Tony Thompson was a top-notch drummer, and although Nile Rodgers was a master of funky chicken-scratch guitar, he was also a nimble player who could make just about anything sound graceful. But the anchor was bassist Bernard Edwards, who is arguably the most influential bassist ever in pop music, even more so than greats like Paul McCartney of the Beatles or James Jamerson of the Motown house band.

Edwards's masterpiece was the slinky, muscular bassline in "Good Times," which was sampled wholesale for "Rapper's Delight" and a host of other hip-hop jams. It was also adapted by Queen a year later for their hit "Another One Bites the Dust." Maybe Queen bassist John Deacon recognized the bassline's power because he was present at its conception. He had been hanging out with Rodgers and making a tour of New York's finest nightclubs, which ended at Chic's recording studio, the Power Station. When they arrived, Edwards was late for the planned session. Rodgers didn't want to look feckless in front of Deacon, so he started showing a song to drummer Tony Thompson, "acting like we planned it that way," Rodgers told me. When Edwards walked in, he didn't apologize; he just plugged in. "He started playing a bassline that was probably really good," Rodgers said—but Rodgers thought it would sound even better if it was a walking bassline. "I was screaming, 'Walk! Walk, motherfucker!'" Edwards began the famous *da-da-dum-*

dum-dum line, and Rodgers started shouting again, at engineer Bob Clearmountain this time: *"Make it red."* Clear- mountain dutifully pushed the record button.

Chic freak out on p. 45 of Chapter 3.

"We got it on the first take," Rodgers proudly reported.

● ● ●

Are members of Monty Python on the Beatles' "Yellow Submarine"? I'm almost certain it's Graham Chapman echoing Ringo in the third verse.

The guests singing in the chorus and adding sound effects did not include any Pythons, but did feature Brian Jones of the Rolling Stones, Marianne Faithfull, and Pattie Boyd Harrison (of "Layla" fame); to produce water noises, John Lennon blew bubbles through a straw in a bucket of water. In 1966, when "Yellow Submarine" was recorded, *Monty Python's Flying Circus* was still three years away. The Beatles were big fans of the show, though; Paul McCartney would stop recording sessions so he could watch, and George Harrison ended up producing several Python films, including *Life of Brian.* (Also a Python watcher: Elvis Presley, who apparently got into the habit of calling people "squire" from Eric Idle's "nudge-nudge" sketch.)

● ● ●

That amazing drum sound on the Ronettes' "Be My Baby"—how did Phil Spector get it?

Bum-ba-bum-BOOM. That bass-drum pattern is possibly the most famous drum opening on any song, and it's constantly used in movies, although never better than in Martin Scorsese's 1973 film *Mean Streets.* The Ronettes' first single was also their biggest, hitting number two in 1963 (kept from the top by Jimmy Gilmer and the Fireballs' "Sugar Shack"). Today, it stands as the most indelible example of Spector's "Wall of Sound" production, which was state of the art from 1961 through 1966.

After "River Deep, Mountain High" flopped, the genius became a recluse; Spector married Ronettes lead singer Ronnie Bennett in 1966 (they divorced in 1974), but otherwise rarely emerged from his Los Angeles mansion, apparently spending his energy over the intervening decades on growing a huge, unkempt mop of gray hair. In 2003, he was charged with murder for shooting actress Lana Clarkson, so when I contacted his representative in 2004 asking about the details of the recording of "Be My Baby," I didn't expect a reply. But a week later, I got an eight-page email from Spector, offering a truckload of previously unrevealed details on studio drummer Hal Blaine and Gold Star Studios, where the song was recorded over a six-month period. Some relevant excerpts from that email (lightly edited, mostly for punctuation):

> I always had ideas for the drum sounds that were different each time. There were times when Hal Blaine would sit for hours, and never play a lick, and/or wait outside the studio while I would get everyone else sounding the way I wanted; I would build instrument by instrument, adding them slowly, on top of each other, with the drums being *last*. And many times, if I couldn't get the right drum sound, at the end of the session, after hours and hours of work, I would cancel the session, even though we had worked four or five or more hours.
>
> The drum sound I had in mind came about fairly quickly this time, albeit many hours after getting a "sound" on all the other musicians. I had the echo in place on everything else, and Gold Star's echo

was a nightmare to handle, as it changed from minute to minute. If someone moved, the echo would change, like the wind. So everyone had to remain as stationary as possible (much to their dismay), or the echo would change the sound I was trying to get. So when Hal Blaine would walk back into the room (because he wouldn't be sitting there the entire four hours), nobody could move a microphone, and he couldn't brush up against anyone, or anyone's microphone. Unlike Motown's studio echo, which was consistent, Gold Star's was not.

But on the day of "Be My Baby," the echo sounded real good, and more important, consistent. You can hear how consistent it is, on the ending of the recording, when I told Hal to solo on all the breaks and fills, which I thought would be very sexual to add to the sound of the recording. The echo was excellent that day: in particular, the echo from the *overhead mike,* which picked up the bass drum beautifully and filled the room up, which is why I decided to use it (the bass drum) as the intro. Normally, the bass drum beginning the recording would not have been loud enough, or big enough, and I worried if it would be loud enough to sustain the band coming in after it until the day the record was released.

Asked what else he remembered about Gold Star, Spector replied,

The fact that everyone caught crabs in the bathroom, from the toilet seat! A "social disease" nobody could talk about in those days. Since I owned my own label, Philles Records, for a laugh I would bring my record distributors down to Gold Star Studios and tell them to use the bathroom, just because I knew they would catch crabs from the toilet seat. Every musician caught it, and their wives and girlfriends from them, and nobody knew where they were getting them from? Boy, I bet those crabs broke up some very sweet—and what could have been long-term—relationships! Imagine coming home with crabs in your pubic area, and the next day your wife asks you where did *she* get them from, in *her* pubic area? When she knows she got them from *you*! And you swear you were working at a Phil Spector session! And you were! And you *have* been "true blue." That's very fucking funny! And every gynecologist and urologist in Los Angeles and Beverly Hills was telling everyone that the *only* way you could catch crabs was from *sexual intercourse*! But that was bullshit. Gold Star had a crab-infested *toilet seat*! I tell you, it was one of the funniest scenarios in the world, watching this crab scene go down over the weeks. Of course, getting rid of those son-of-a-bitch crabs was no picnic! And pissing in the parking lot wasn't too "cool" either! The studio had mice and roaches as well. It never would have passed any health-code test. But who the fuck cared? It had a great echo chamber. Inconsistent, and a nightmare to use, but fucking great. So, all in all, I think everyone would agree that Gold Star's erratic but sensational echo chamber, and the wonderful memories of that studio, were well worth the price of the doctor's visits and the Quell lotion it took to cure all the crabs we caught there!

13 SAY MY NAME, SAY MY NAME

Rock 'n' Roll Nomenclature

Starting a band is work. Not as much work as mowing lawns, admittedly. But learning to play an instrument well enough that you can recruit some friends or strangers to join you? Work. Finding a place to rehearse, and then later having the audacity to charge people to listen to you? Work. (Maybe that's why Throwing Muses, in their early days, gave a dollar to anyone who came to one of their shows.) But coming up with a name for your band? That's the fun part—which is why thousands of bands have never made it out of the name-creation and logo-design stage. (The logo-design laboratory is often the back cover of a school notebook.) My nonexistent band in eighth grade? Graven Images (without any *the* before the name—I was going through a major Talking Heads phase).

● ● ●

*H*O**W** did Iggy Pop get his name?

Born James Newell Osterberg, he drummed for a band called the Iguanas in high school; a shortening of their name gave him the Iggy handle. When he was living with the rest of the Stooges in Ann Arbor, Michigan, experimenting with drugs and the sonic possibilities of vacuum cleaners, he was called Iggy Stooge and Iggy Osterberg. He didn't acquire the last name Pop until he shaved off his eyebrows; the band had a friend named Jimmy Pop who had lost all his hair, including his eyebrows, so Iggy got tagged with his name. (Iggy said he picked it because it sounded good for show business.) When the Stooges played their first show for a paying crowd, on March 3, 1968, Iggy painted his face like a mime's, wore an antique nightshirt, and built himself an Afro with aluminum foil. That night, he learned an answer

to one of mankind's imponderable questions:
"What are eyebrows are good for?" The answer is
"keeping sweat out of your eyes"; by the end of
the gig, so much sweat and oil and glitter had
dripped down Iggy's forehead, his eyes had
become severely swollen.

● ● ●

My friend had a weird dream: It
revealed to him that Jimmy Eat World chose their
name because they were Jewish (the initials are
J.E.W.). Could there be any truth to this, or has
my friend just smoked himself retarded?

I can't specifically comment on your friend's IQ,
but Jimmy Eat World are goyim. Drummer Zach
Lind told me, "None of us are Jewish, and the
name has nothing to do with any religious or
social positioning. It's totally coincidental." The
name actually came from an ongoing fight
between two of guitarist Tom Linton's brothers.
The smaller one, Ed, was tired of being picked on
by the heftier one, Jimmy, so he retaliated with a
crayon drawing of Jimmy shoving the entire globe
down his gullet, captioned JIMMY EAT WORLD. Lind
said, "We chose it because we thought it was a
funny name, but we've regretted that decision
ever since."

• • •

What's the meaning

behind the name of The E Street Band?

Bruce Springsteen had played in many bands, with names such as Steel Mill and Dr. Zoom and the Sonic Boom, but when he signed his record contract, he did it as a solo artist. When he went on tour behind *Greetings from Asbury Park, N.J.,* he had just five guys backing him up, and they didn't even have a name; on some 1974 posters, the act is billed as BRUCE SPRINGSTEEN AND BAND. As original keyboardist David Sancious remembered it, "We needed a name." On a long drive back from a show, the group brainstormed names for hours, without anything clicking. By the time they got back to the Jersey shore, it was daylight. They were headed for the house of Sancious's family, where the band sometimes practiced. The address: 1105 E Street, Belmar, New Jersey. Spring-steen saw a street sign and started saying it over and over: "E Street, E Street. E Street Band. Yeah." That Belmar neighborhood had another name that Springsteen made famous. A nearby cross-street

Where else does Springsteen visit in his lyrics? The list's on p. 131 of Chapter 10.

was Tenth Avenue—later to be known for its
freeze-outs.

• • •

I was just wondering:
What does t.A.T.u. stand for? I heard it's short for
Teens Against Tobacco Use, but t.A.T.u. don't
really seem like the type of girls who are against
smoking.

When it comes to the world of pseudo-lesbian
Russian teenagers in schoolgirl outfits, nothing
is as it seems. But in fact, Lena Katina and Julia
Volkova, the girls who performed the hit single
"All the Things She Said," took their name from
a shortened version of the Russian phrase
pronounced "Ta lyhubit tu" (I'll spare you the
Cyrillic, but it translates as "This girl is loving
that one"). There is *also* an organization called
Teens Against Tobacco Use (TATU), who don't
sing, but rather offer up such statements as "I
use my commitment to be tobacco-free to teach
children to make the healthy choice not to
smoke." In contrast, the pop duo favors maxims
such as "We are singing about our love. Love
between girl and girl."

• • •

What does DMX stand for?

The inspiration wasn't Dark Man X or Da Mutant Xavier. The name on the rapper's birth certificate was Earl Simmons, but around age sixteen, when he started beatboxing and rapping at the group home where he was living, he decided he needed a new name. He found it on the Oberheim DMX drum machine. "Since I felt I was nice by the beats, I took that," DMX said. "It was strong, powerful. I liked the three letters and thought that it would be cool to make them stand for different things . . . I was no longer Earl Simmons or even Crazy Earl. I was DMX. *DMX The Beat Box Enforcer.*"

● ● ●

Where did Pearl Jam get their name?

There's a lot of misinformation on this subject, most of it gleefully spread by the band. For example, despite Eddie Vedder's repeated claims, he did not have a great-grandmother named Pearl who married a Native American and cooked up jam with peyote as an ingredient. And although the band was originally named Mookie Blaylock, after the star NBA point guard, "Pearl Jam" was not his nickname. (They changed their name to avoid legal problems, but the title of their debut album, *Ten,* was also Blaylock's jersey number.) The band also doesn't seem to have intended their name to refer to semen. So why did they pick it? They just liked the word *pearl:* It's surfer slang for submerging the nose of your board, it's the title of a good Janis Joplin record, it was the nickname of basketball great Earl Monroe, and Vedder *did* have a cool great-grandmother named Pearl. She didn't wed a Native American, but she did marry a circus contortionist. So a Pearl Jam might be a Monroe slam-dunk or, as Vedder said he prefers to think of it, the creative conflict that turns the grain of sand in an oyster into a jewel.

● ● ●

Has R.E.M. ever performed under any other name?

At their very first show, they were known as Twisted Kites. Later, R.E.M. often employed pseudonyms for secret gigs, such as The Mystery Twins, It Crawled from the South, Bingo Hand Job, and Hornets Attack Victor Mature. The band's members also have participated in dozens of other projects, ranging from the Hindu Love Gods (Peter Buck, Mike Mills, and Bill Berry playing drunken covers with Warren Zevon) to 1066 Gaggle O' Sound (Michael Stipe doing a one-man show on a Farfisa organ—so dubbed because 1066 was Stipe's "favorite year in history").

● ● ●

Just how did Weezer get their name?

A quick history of the names that Rivers Cuomo has used for his bands: His high-school metal act was called Avant Garde; they moved to Los Angeles and then changed their name to Zoom (rejecting the options Prong and Power Chicken). After they broke up, Cuomo joined Sixty Wrong Sausages, which in early 1992 evolved into a nameless quartet. While they wrote songs and rehearsed, this group considered Meathead, Outhouse, Hummingbird, The Big Jones, and This Niblet. Then came their break: Keanu Reeves's band, Dogstar, decided to play an impromptu gig at Raji's Bar and Rib Shack on Hollywood Boulevard. An opening band was needed that night; Cuomo's group lucked into the show, but needed a real name. Cuomo nominated Weezer—a nickname given to him when he was a kid, by other children who were teasing him about his asthma. The band had a long meeting and kicked around many more names, but nobody could come up with anything

Instructions for Weezer's secret treasure map is on p. 19 of Chapter 1.

better, and Cuomo stuck to his guns (or, rather, his inhaler).

● ● ●

Is it true that the Foo Fighters' original name was the Food Fighters, but at an early show the venue didn't have a D to use on the sign?

Sadly, no; Dave Grohl chose the band's name and recorded the debut album before playing any live shows. *Foo fighters* is actually an old term for UFOs; World War II pilots reported seeing odd balls of light that circled around their planes, and borrowed a catchphrase from the comic-strip character Smokey Stover (whose creator, Bill Holman, littered his strip with the nonsense word *foo,* in phrases like "A man's foo is his castle" and "Foo-losophy"). Although Grohl has warned that "that UFO

Does Dave Grohl's chewing gum lose its flavor when he leaves it on the bedpost overnight? See p. 9 of Chapter 1.

stuff is all overblown," he is sufficiently interested in flying-saucer conspiracies to have named his label Roswell Records (after the site where the aliens allegedly landed) and to have taken a walk-on role on *The X-Files.* If Grohl had chosen another term for the same aerial phenomena, his band would have been called the Kraut Fireballs.

● ● ●

Where did Velvet Revolver

get their name? Weren't they called the Project?

The band, also briefly known as Reloaded, didn't decide on a name until the last possible moment. In fact, their songs in *Hulk* and *The Italian Job* are credited to "Scott Weiland, Slash, Duff McKagan, Matt Sorum and Dave Kushner," which is a bit of a mouthful for a DJ back-announcing a single.

"Coming up with a name was an eventuality we were dreading," McKagan told me. "We were like, we *have* to come up with a fuckin' name." After seeing a movie financed by Revolution Studios, Slash suggested Revolver, and the band liked it because of the Beatles reference. "But I did a Google search on *revolver* and there was like a thousand bands, so that was impossible," McKagan said. They started toying with different versions, and Weiland came up with Black Velvet

Revolver, which was deemed too close in cadence to Stone Temple Pilots. Truncated, however, it made everyone happy. McKagan swore that nobody involved with the band realized there was a firearm overlap in the names of Guns N' Roses and Velvet Revolver until it was too late.

● ● ●

Did the Circle Jerks and the Gun Club really trade names?

Almost. Circa 1980, two pivotal figures in the Los Angeles underground music scene were roommates: Jeffrey Lee Pierce had a band called Creeping Ritual; sharing a bathroom with him was Keith Morris, lead singer for the legendary hardcore band Black Flag. Alongside acts such as the Cramps and X, Pierce was helping to define the roots-punk sound of the L.A. scene, performing gigs mostly at Chinese restaurants. But after one show, Pierce was worried that he had pissed off the club's management sufficiently for the band to get blacklisted there. The easiest move was to change his group's name. (This also had the advantage of shedding the goth connotations of Creeping Ritual.) The Gun Club, the band's new name, was indeed suggested by his roommate Morris. But although Morris was leaving Black

Flag and starting a new band of his own, Pierce didn't suggest its name (the Circle Jerks). His half of the trade: the lyrics to the song "Group Sex," which became the title track for the Circle Jerks' debut album.

● ● ●

Why does Jay-Z call himself Hova?

It's a play on Jay-Hova, or Jehovah, one of the Old Testament names of God. Jay-Z (born Shawn Carter) got the nickname back in 1993, when he borrowed studio time and was recording some of his first tracks. The other people in the studio marveled to discover that Jay-Z was improvising all his lyrics, and decided that his ability was nothing short of miraculous. So they dubbed him J-Hova. Like Eric Clapton decades before him, Jay-Z resisted being anointed as the Creator. "I've never been comfortable being called God," Jay-Z has said. "I shorten it to Hova." Which isn't that modest, actually, but if anybody's earned it, he has. As he puts it on his song "Breathe Easy (Lyrical Exercise)": "I'm far from being God / But I work goddamn hard."

14 LONG BLACK VEIL

We have two ways of memorializing rock stars who die young: compilation discs and conspiracy theories. Neither method, however, provides an adequate answer as to why so many of them expire in their twenty-seventh year on the planet. Kurt Cobain, Jimi Hendrix, Robert Johnson, Janis Joplin, Jim Morrison—all dead at twenty-seven. And that's just the A team; other rockers who made it through just one score and seven include Chris Bell of Big Star, D. Boon of the Minutemen, and Pigpen of the Grateful Dead. That's old enough to have left their mark, yet young enough that we can always argue about whether they would have been able to outdo themselves if they had lived.

● ● ●

I heard that in college, some friends of James Taylor's flew his girlfriend in as a surprise, but her plane crashed—which is what "Fire and Rain" is based on. Any truth to that story?

Only a little. "Fire and Rain" was inspired by the death of a female friend of Taylor's, Susie Schnerr. But Taylor never went to college, Schnerr wasn't a romantic interest, and tragically, Schnerr committed suicide. Taylor's friends didn't tell him she had died until six months later because they didn't want to rattle him while he was recording *Sweet Baby James*—hence the song's line "They let me know you were gone." Taylor wrote the first verse of "Fire and Rain" in his basement apartment in London, the second verse in a New York City hospital where he was hospitalized because of his heroin addiction, and the third verse in a Massachusetts psychiatric clinic.

● ● ●

My roommate told me that Jeff Porcaro, drummer for Toto, actually died in a "tragic gardening accident," à la *Spinal Tap*. Can that be true?

Porcaro—who was also a top studio drummer, with such credits as Steely Dan, Michael Jackson, and Bruce Springsteen on his résumé—keeled over suddenly on August 5, 1992, when he was just thirty-eight years old. The initial report from Toto's record label was that Porcaro had expired because of an allergic reaction to pesticide while spraying his garden—which, bizarrely, would indeed qualify as a tragic gardening accident. A month later, however, the coroner's report revealed that there was no pesticide in his bloodstream. The cause was actually a heart attack due to hardened arteries from his extensive use of cocaine. This, of course, provokes further questions: What sick minds cooked up a *Spinal Tap* alibi for Porcaro's death? And why didn't they claim instead that he had spontaneously combusted or choked on somebody else's vomit? I grilled a source close to the band. He requested anonymity but insisted that the initial report wasn't a coverup of a drug binge, just a mistaken conclusion reached when Porcaro abruptly died in his garden.

● ● ●

I heard that the former bassist of Iron Butterfly was an innovative scientist who was killed after finding out in his research that objects could go faster than light. Is this true? It seems pretty bizarre.

Philip "Taylor" Kramer, born in 1952, joined an Iron Butterfly reunion in 1974 and recorded two forgotten albums with the band (whose "In-A-Gadda-Da-Vida" heyday was some years behind them by then). When the group broke up again in 1977, he got an engineering degree, worked on the MX missile, and later specialized in video compression.

In early 1995, Kramer said that he had developed a formula for instantaneous transmission of matter, exciting anyone who ever wanted a *Star Trek* transporter. You might want to consider his claim with some skepticism, though; around the same time, he also said that the earth was about to be consumed by a supernova and that his wife was actually Mother Earth. On February 12, Kramer called 9-1-1 from Los Angeles International Airport, told the operator he was going to kill himself and that "O.J. is innocent," and then vanished. His disappearance fueled talk of foul play or alien abduction—until 1999, when hikers found Kramer's body at the bottom of a two-hundred-foot ravine in Malibu, California. The evidence suggests that Kramer had become mentally unbalanced and, tragically, had made good on his threats of suicide.

● ● ●

Did one of the Temptations die in a crackhouse?

No—he *overdosed* at the crackhouse, but died in the hospital. On June 1, 1991, three weeks after a Temptations reunion tour, lead singer David Ruffin reportedly smoked ten vials of crack and passed out. A limousine dropped him off at the Hospital of the University of Pennsylvania; the driver identified his passenger and drove away without giving his own name. An hour later, Ruffin expired. He had been wearing a money belt containing $40,000, which was stolen sometime during the night of his death and never recovered. Since Ruffin died broke, Michael Jackson paid for his funeral.

● ● ●

Before Ty Longley of Great White, did any rock stars die onstage?

Yes, although this is not as great an occupational hazard for musicians as drugs or traveling in small airplanes. Among the notables who had fatal heart attacks in front of live crowds: blues legend Johnny "Guitar" Watson, Country Dick Montana of the Beat Farmers, novelty artist Tiny Tim, British skinhead ska star Judge Dread, and Mark Sandman of Morphine. (Some people think soul legend Jackie Wilson died onstage after his heart attack. In fact, he survived for eight more years, although he spent them in a coma.) In addition, Les Harvey, guitarist for the Scottish soul band Stone the Crows, was electrocuted onstage in 1972. But punk rocker G. G. Allin, who spent most of his career threatening to commit suicide onstage, actually died in a New York City apartment of a heroin overdose.

● ● ●

Did the Yardbirds' Keith Relf really get electrocuted onstage by an electric guitar?

No, it was in the privacy of his own home. Relf was the singer of the Yardbirds for six years while an array of star guitarists (Eric Clapton, Jeff Beck,

Jimmy Page) rotated through the ranks. When he died on May 14, 1976, it was widely reported that he had been playing electric guitar in the bathtub and electrocuted himself. (Other places it's unwise to play an electric guitar: on a tall building during a thunderstorm, in front of an oncoming freight train, at the Newport Folk Festival.) In fact, his family says, Relf was not in the tub; apparently he was playing guitar in the basement when the tragic combination of malfunctioning equipment, an exposed pipe, and electric current killed him at age thirty-three.

● ● ●

I got interested in Donny Hathaway after I heard Ruben Studdard was a big fan, and I was wondering: Did he commit suicide?

Hathaway was a soul singer/songwriter best known for his duets with Roberta Flack; their hit cover of James Taylor's "You've Got a Friend" led them to do two whole albums together. Tragically, on January 13, 1979, Hathaway fell to his death from the fifteenth floor of the Essex House Hotel. There was no note, meaning nobody will ever know for sure what thoughts were going through Hathaway's head, but he *had* been hospitalized for depression. The coroner ruled his death a suicide. Jesse Jackson delivered the eulogy at Hathaway's funeral and, noting that Hathaway had been dressed for the New York winter in a coat and scarf, contended that no one gets bundled up "just to jump out of a window." Further evidence suggesting the fall was accidental: Hathaway had been cheerful earlier the same day, while in the studio with Flack. Furthermore, he was in the habit of leaning out the window of his seventeenth-floor apartment in Chicago, preaching and singing to passersby on the street below. Since he had been tossed out of other hotels for the same habit, it seems possible that it was a repeat of that dangerous behavior that led to his untimely plummet.

● ● ●

Did Johnny Ace really shoot himself?

Ace, famous for his smooth baritone and the single "Pledging My Love," was a popular ballad singer in the early '50s, and routinely jammed on piano with B. B. King. On Christmas Day 1954, he died of a gunshot wound backstage at Houston's City Auditorium between sets of a show with Big Mama Thornton. The coroner's verdict was Russian roulette, but some people speculate that Ace was shot by Don Robey, owner of Duke

Records, in an effort to end contract renegotiations. (Robey was a music-world thug who was known for pulling guns during business transactions.) The more likely story, corroborated by several eyewitnesses, is that although Ace wasn't playing Russian roulette, he was horsing around with his own gun and accidentally shot himself— or, as a Houston homicide detective on the scene that night put it, he died of "pistolitis."

• • •

Did Keith Moon and Mama Cass really die in the same apartment?

Bizarrely, yes; both died in a flat in London's Mayfair district owned by their mutual friend, singer-songwriter Harry Nilsson. Since Nilsson was only in London half the year, he would loan the apartment to pals while he was out of town. "It was just a typical London flat," Nilsson said, "but it was in a great neighborhood. It was across from the Playboy Club, diagonally. From one balcony you could read the time from Big Ben, and from the other balcony you could watch the Bunnies go up and down."

"Mama" Cass Elliot, best known as one of the Mamas and the Papas, was in town for a live performance when she died on July 29, 1974.

Although it was widely reported that she choked on a ham sandwich, the autopsy revealed that she actually died of a heart attack. Her cardiac condition may have been exacerbated by an extreme yo-yo diet, where she would alternate weeklong fasts with massive weight gain.

Four years later, Keith Moon, the Who drummer legendary for his excess, was borrowing the apartment from Nilsson. On September 6, 1978, he attended a screening of the movie *The Buddy Holly Story,* hosted by Paul McCartney. At 4:30 A.M., he came home and swallowed a handful of Heminevrin sleeping pills while watching the Vincent Price horror movie *The Abominable Dr. Phibes.* A few hours later he woke up, cooked himself a steak, and swallowed it down, along with some champagne and more pills. He then passed out again, dying sometime that day of an accidental overdose. The autopsy revealed he had taken thirty-two Heminevrin pills. Understandably spooked, Nilsson never returned to his apartment; Pete Townshend, who had been renting it from him on Moon's behalf, bought it from him so he wouldn't ever have to see it again. In 2002, when Townshend was asked what he would say to Keith Moon in the afterlife, his joking answer was, "You owe me five thousand pounds back rent."

15

DO YOU WANT TO KNOW A SECRET?

Rock's Great Imponderables

During the years that I worked on the column that became this book, there were some questions I never answered. Some were too mundane, some too specialized. But a few always seemed just out of my reach. The one I always regretted not being able to nail down to my desired standards of accuracy was "Which rock stars wear toupees?"

The question has an elementary beauty; with so many rock stars over sixty, *of course* there must be some whose youthful manes have long abandoned them. While Elton John grinned his way through the public humiliation of getting new hair plugs, there are likely some who are trying to stay secretly youthful and vigorous. (This particular species of vanity can be found more in lead singers and guitarists; rhythm-section members seem more inclined to let nature take its course.)

One source told me the (unconfirmed) story of an American folk-rock star touring England in the '70s. A London barber was summoned to a hotel room to cut the star's hair. At the appointed time, he showed up with his scissors and other accoutrements. When he knocked on the door, he was greeted by a road manager and told the star wasn't present. "But I have an appointment to cut his hair," the barber stammered. "Oh!" said the road manager. "His *hair*'s here." The barber was escorted inside and introduced to the star's wig, which he relieved of a few stray hairs.

When David Bowie was touring with Moby on the Area2 Festival, I went to the Jones Beach Theater, just outside New York City, and interviewed him about the day's events. He offered polite quotes about Moby and Busta Rhymes. Then, after I had the material I needed for my story, I asked him which rock stars wear hair-pieces. For the first time during our conversation, his eyes lit up and he leaned forward. "Why do you want to know?" he asked.

I explained, painting my pursuit of knowledge in the most high-minded tones possible. He grinned, and reflected. "Ohhh," he said, clearly bursting with the desire to gossip, "I shouldn't." So the toupee question will have to wait for another day—one of many questions that will get answered when Bowie finally spills all—but this chapter contains the answers to some of the other eternal mysteries of rock.

● ● ●

Did Robert Johnson sell his soul to the devil?

Some questions are purely theological: Can one actually barter one's soul to the devil for guitar lessons? If so, do the infernal exchange rates fluctuate? Can Joe Satriani ask for a refund? So when we consider the story of legendary bluesman Robert Johnson (1911–1938), it's more useful to ask whether Johnson believed he made such a deal, or whether he wanted other people to think he had. You won't find much evidence of a supernatural bargain in his music. Although Johnson recorded a few songs with satanic references—including the memorable, atypical "Hellhound on My Trail"—other contemporary blues singers, such as Bessie Smith, sang many more such numbers without people concluding they had encountered Satan at the metaphysical swap meet.

Scholars have recently pinpointed the origin of the myth, which started decades after Johnson's death. In a 1965 interview, blues guitarist Son House told the story of how he knew Johnson when he was a good harmonica player but a terrible guitarist; between House's sets at juke joints, Johnson would borrow House's guitar and "drive the people nuts." The next time House saw Johnson, he was much better; as House told the story, the improvement took only six months, although later research has revealed it had to be at least two or three times that long.

When House's tale was reprinted a year later, a postscript (probably inaccurate) had been appended, quoting House as saying that Johnson made a deal with the devil. From there, the tale kept getting "improved," until the Faustian bargain became an indelible part of Johnson's image. But the people who actually knew Johnson in the '30s, such as his frequent traveling companion Johnny Shines, scoffed at the notion that Johnson had sold his soul, or even suggested he had. "He never told me that lie, no," Shines said. "If he would have, I'd have called him a liar right to his face."

• • •

His lack of compositional abilities aside, is Ringo Starr generally considered as a drummer:

A. A very talented instrumentalist whose abilities are/were underestimated?

B. A not-bad musician elevated by his good fortune in winding up a Beatle?

C. A pretty lame musician by comparison not just to his bandmates but to most of his contemporaries in successful rock bands?

I have thought both B and C at various points, but heard (possibly fulsome/insincere) testimony to A. Help me out!

A huge caveat: Answering this question requires more subjectivity than most of the others in the book do, so you might not agree with the next few paragraphs, even though I'm right. Conventional wisdom has historically oscillated between B and C among all but the most devoted Beatlemaniacs, but lately, more people would opt for A. (Paul McCartney has also gone through a long-term critical resurgence, possibly because he no longer gets lightweight but massively successful ballads on the radio, so people can remember why they liked him in the first place. But that's another story.) Personally, I would say the truth lies somewhere between A and B, and if you made me pick one option, I'd plump for A.

Starr was the least nimble instrumentalist in the Beatles, and he wasn't flashy, but his great virtue was his impeccable timing, which is the single most important quality in any drummer. He was always in the pocket, always laid down a solid groove, and never got in the way of the other performances. Sure, lots of other drummers had more chops, but that doesn't mean that, say, Charlie Watts (to pick a random excellent rock drummer with jazz training) could have done a better job playing on those Beatles tracks.

Let's check in with Lenny Kravitz, another underrated drummer: "Next to Ringo, I like [Stevie Wonder] best. Both of those guys are very lyrical drummers. They're the kind of drummers that a lot of other drummers just don't get. Like I hear musicians say, 'Yeah, Ringo can't play.' You know what? *Fuck you.* Because you obviously have no ears at all. Ringo was so sick, it was ridiculous. I mean, nobody played a tom solo like Ringo."

A few Beatles tracks where Starr really shines, and worth listening to while just paying attention to the drums, are "Drive My Car," where he's particularly inventive on the breaks; "Ticket to Ride," where he basically invents heavy-metal drumming; and "Rain," where he's playing like a man possessed. The "Strawberry Fields Forever" outtakes on the *Anthology 2* collection also show him doing some really interesting stuff (basically inventing the trip-hop beat).

Also, Ringo had star power (no pun intended). As John Lennon said, "Whatever that spark is in Ringo, we all know it, but we can't put our finger on it. Whether it's acting, drumming, or singing, I don't know. There's something in him that is projectable and he would have surfaced as an individual." That doesn't really add to his value as a drummer, but it certainly added to his value as a Beatle.

● ● ●

Did Mick Jagger get good grades at the London School of Economics?

No, although he probably could have. According to Walter Stern, Jagger's tutor at the LSE, Jagger started as a promising student in October 1961. "He announced his intention of going into business but was worried about mathematics," Stern remembered. Almost immediately, however, Jagger ran into Keith Richards and got distracted by blues music. He started cutting his classes, some of which started at the un-rock hour of ten A.M.; when he took his exams in June 1962, he got straight Cs. (The subjects were economics, British government, economic history, political history, and English legal institutions.) Nevertheless, he dutifully returned the following academic year, even working in the library—hedging his bets until the Rolling Stones had a contract to record their first single in May 1963, at which point he left school. "My father was furious with me," Jagger said. "But I really didn't like being at college. It wasn't like it was Oxford and it had been the most wonderful time of my life. It was really a dull, boring course I was stuck on."

● ● ●

I was listening to Kid Rock's "Cowboy," and I wondered, what *are* the right reasons to open an escort service?

The line is Rock's fantasy about life on the West Coast. After rhyming *scotch* with *crotch,* he distills his pimp aspirations: "open an escort service for all the right reasons / And set up shop at the top of the Four Seasons." Asked what the right reasons for opening an escort service are, Rock responded not with noble claims of helping wayward girls or reducing chlamydia outbreaks, but rather, "Awww. That's just a silly line. There's no deep thought process behind it. To get paid. To make money. Isn't that what everything is the right reason for?" Not to overanalyze a comedic line, but it's interesting how little space there is in Kid Rock's world between the right reasons and the wrong reasons.

● ● ●

What the hell did Billie Joe McAllister throw off the Tallahatchee Bridge?

More than thirty-five years after the release of Bobbie Gentry's "Ode to Billie Joe" in 1967, questions linger about her haunting southern-gothic ballad. (Decades from now, will anyone still wonder who let the dogs out?) Gentry's number one single tells the story of a family dinner where the narrator finds out that her boyfriend, Billie Joe McCallister, has jumped off the Tallahatchee Bridge; the day before, people spotted her and Billie Joe throwing an unidentified object off that same bridge. "Everybody has a different guess about what was thrown off the bridge: flowers, a ring, even a baby," Gentry has said. "What was thrown off the bridge really isn't that important. The message of the song, if there must be a message, revolves around the nonchalant way the family talks about the suicide. The song is a study in unconscious cruelty." Sinead O'Connor's 1995 cover version didn't shed much light on the song's mysteries, but the 1976 movie adaptation, *Ode to Billy Joe* (with Robby Benson in the title role), provided some answers. They seem like arbitrary inventions of the filmmakers, but they're the closest thing the song has to an official "solution": In the movie, Billy Joe tosses his girlfriend Bobbie Lee's rag doll off the bridge and then jumps the following day, tormented by uncertainty over his sexual identity.

● ● ●

Doesn't Pete Townshend hurt his hand when he does that windmill thing on the guitar?

Even worse than you think. During a 1989 Who concert in Seattle, Townshend missed the encore when he sliced open his hand on his guitar strings and was rushed to the hospital. During another show that year, Townshend actually impaled his right palm on the guitar's whammy bar. Plus, the guitar strings routinely get underneath his fingernails and rip them off. This means he starts to bleed, and of course, when the guitar pick gets bloody, it becomes slippery and hard to hold. "It is terribly painful," Townshend said in 1994. But he relishes it: "I think, 'This is it. I've arrived. It is the place where I should be, like a boxer in the middle of a fight.' " Of course, before his painful hearing loss, he used to take the same pleasure in how physically punishing the Who's loud amplifiers were; there's clearly a masochistic element to his onstage abandon.

● ● ●

Did Dr. Hook & the Medicine Show ever make it to the cover of *Rolling Stone*?

In 1972, cartoonist and songwriter Shel Silverstein visited Dr. Hook & the Medicine Show in the studio with a question: Would they like to be on the cover of *Rolling Stone*? Since they were struggling for a hit, they said absolutely, although they couldn't imagine how he would manage the trick. Silverstein then proceeded to play them "Cover of the Rolling Stone," a complaint song for jaded rock stars who haven't yet achieved their dream of appearing on the front page of the publication: "We got all the friends that money can buy, so we'll never have to be alone / And we keep gettin' richer but we can't get our picture on the cover of the *Rolling Stone*." Guitarist Rik Elswit remembered, "The dope being excellent, we were in no shape to really evaluate the song. So after we picked ourselves up off the floor and stifled most of the laughing, we went right about recording it." About three hours later, they had recorded a hit single, which peaked at number six. In March 1973, the magazine did feature the band on its cover, albeit with a cartoon of just three of their seven members and the caption WHAT'S-THEIR-NAMES MAKE THE COVER.

Since the song's lyrics had promised "gonna buy five copies for my mother," three members of the band visited the *Rolling Stone* offices in San Francisco and demanded those five copies. "We were in full hippie regalia, with about thirty pounds of hair between the three of us," Elswit said. "The receptionist didn't know who we were or why we were there, and, furthermore, didn't much care. We were frostily informed that we could buy some from the dispenser machines downstairs. At that point, somebody came out of one of the offices, recognized us, and we all had a good laugh—except for the receptionist, who still didn't care. They then produced exactly five copies, and we were escorted out to the street."

● ● ●

Did Bob Dylan really have a motorcycle accident, or was he covering something up?

Something happened on July 29, 1966. *The New York Times* broke the news a few days later: Dylan had been in a motorcycle accident and would be canceling his concert at the Yale Bowl. If you ever wondered whether rumors spread before the Internet, the answer is yes—fans traded stories that Dylan was horribly scarred, paraplegic, insane, or even dead. These stories proved not to be true, but one thing was certain: He was gone.

Dylan spent the next nine months in seclusion in upstate New York; as he recovered, he and the Band made the much-bootlegged music that would ultimately be released as *The Basement Tapes.* He didn't put out a new album until 1968, the deliberately low-key *John Wesley Harding.* So what actually went down that July day? The facts are fuzzy, but the gist appears to be that Dylan visited the home of his manager Albert Grossman in Bearsville, New York. There, Dylan picked up an old Triumph 55 motorcycle and was planning to ride it to a nearby repair shop. As he left the property, however, he took a spill. This is the way he told the story in 1967: "The back wheel locked up, I think. I lost control, swerving from left to right. Next thing I know I was in someplace I never heard of—Middletown, I think—with my face cut up, so I got some scars, and my neck busted up pretty good." The official story at the time was that he broke some vertebrae in his neck, was knocked unconscious, and was in critical condition for a week.

Later, however, witnesses—including Albert Grossman's wife, Sally, famous as the girl on the cover of *Bringing It All Back Home*—would tell the tale differently. Apparently, Dylan had poor eyesight and was notorious for his lack of skill on the bike; as he left the Grossman property, he just lost his balance and fell off the motorcycle in an undignified fashion. Although he could have been driven to a nearby hospital, he was instead taken to a doctor who was an hour away.

Rumors circulated that he was secretly in rehab for drug addiction, but the accident appears to have been genuine, if not as serious as was reported. Afterward, people spotted Dylan in a neck brace, and friends reported that he took up swimming and received ultrasound treatment.

So why did Dylan check out for so long? By 1966, he was not just hailed as the voice of a generation, he was expected to lead folk and rock fans in a new direction with every album and, very possibly, to redefine contemporary society as a hippie utopia. Plus, Dylan had been going virtually nonstop for a long time; he released five records in just over two years, from 1964 to early 1966. He had a full tour of sixty concerts scheduled, plus a contract renegotiation with Columbia Records. Fans and biographers have long assumed that Dylan seized on his injuries—real, if not as serious as reported—as an opportunity to step away from his white-hot celebrity and the pressure that came along with it.

Dylan said as much himself in 2004, in the first volume of his excellent autobiography, *Chronicles:* "I had been in a motorcycle accident and I'd been hurt, but I recovered. Truth was that I wanted to get out of the rat race."

● ● ●

What do those symbols on the cover of *Led Zeppelin IV* represent?

Led Zeppelin decided to leave their 1971 album untitled, although they later conceded that *Led Zeppelin IV* is probably the easiest name for it. (People have sometimes called it "Zoso," "Atlantic SD 7208," or "The Artist Formerly Known as Prince.") Jimmy Page decided that each member should pick a symbol to represent himself, and that those four symbols would serve as the album's title. Robert Plant claims that his (the feather in the circle) was from "the ancient Mu civilization which existed about fifteen thousand years ago as part of a lost continent somewhere in the Pacific Ocean between China and Mexico." John Paul Jones picked his (the encircled petals) out of a book of runes (early Gaelic writing), because it signified somebody who is confident and competent. John Bonham picked his (the three circles) out of the same book because he liked the way it looked; later, the band realized it was also the logo for Ballantine beer. Page has remained mum on his glyph, saying only that he designed it himself and it's not supposed to be the word *Zoso*. (Asked the meaning by a fan after a 1994 appearance on an Australian talk show, Page allegedly replied, cryptically, "Frying tonight." Which might just have meant he was heading for a post-show burger.) He did once, however, divulge the true meaning to Plant, who later lamented, "Would you believe that I have since forgotten what it was and now Pagey won't tell me?"

For more information on many different rock 'n' roll acts, turn to p. 1 and start reading the book again.

ACKNOWLEDGMENTS

My heartfelt thanks to everyone who asked me the music-related questions in this book, usually via email but sometimes in person. For those about to rock, I salute you: Angela Allen, Chris Allsopp, Sameer Anaokar, Tim Atkinson, Dennis Austin, Paul B., Tom Baltzer, Jill Booth-Clibborn, Rob Brendle, Matthew Brooks, Chris Bubeck, Susan Ann Burrows, Joey C., Kathi Chastain, Mike Costanzo, Andre Dementiev, Soren deSelby, Steve Doberstein, Andy Erdman, Sara Fenchel, Ted Friedman, Stephen L. Garbin, Paul Gerardi, Sandy Gillespie, Kevin Grady, Joe Greene, Wendy Greene, Ola Hacansson, Allen Hege, Scott Hess, Joe Hobaica, Mollie Hogan, Dan

Huddleston, Jeremiah Johnson, Erin Joyner, Kevin Lang, Will Levith, Colin Lingle, Kerry MacLaine, Niko Matsarakias, Mark McClusky, Angus McDonald, Jeffrey P. McManus, Krisha Mendoza, John Mitcham, Debra Morrow, R. Dyche Mullins, Mike Nawrocki, Darcy Nickless, John Nienart, Lawton Outlaw, LaShondra Parris, Zooey Parry, B. Perkins, Doug Perry, Laura Proctor, Alexis Richel, Bob Rossney, Kerry Roth, Wendy Roth, Bob Ruggiero, Christian Ruzich, Teresa Samuels, Adam Satariano, Rob Schell, Dave Scott, Rob Sheffield, Ben Smith, Dan Sorrell, Dennis Strome, Cynthia Sudul, Nyssa Tang, Mark Tennenhouse, Bill Tipper, Stephanie Vardavas, Tonya Varner, Mike Walsh, Amanda Williams, and Miriam Zellnik. This book wouldn't exist without their questions. Similarly, dozens of musicians and other people in the music business not only tolerated my impertinent queries, but responded with details and good humor. This book would have been impoverished without their generosity, and I thank them.

If you have music questions of your own, you can send them to me at askmrrock@gmail.com. If there's ever a sequel to this book (*I Still Know What Elton's Little John Did Last Summer,* maybe, or *Tiny Dancer 2: Electric Boogaloo*), I'll answer as many as I can. (If you think you've spotted an error in these pages, please let me know at the same address.) And if you have burning questions about the film world, send them to me at askmrmovies@gmail.com, and I'll see what I can do. (For announcements and other writing by me, you can always check my Web site at www.gavinedwards.com.)

This book started as a column at *Rolling Stone,* the magazine I am proud to call home. Thanks to all the editors at *Rolling Stone* whom I have been lucky enough to work with over the past few years: Nathan Brackett, Jason Fine, Jim Kaminsky, Joe Levy, Kirk Miller, Tom Nawrocki, David Swanson, Peter Travers, and Sean Woods—plus, of course, editor and publisher Jann S. Wenner, without whom none of this would have been possible.

I would also like to thank everyone in the *Rolling Stone* research department, especially those who were on staff when these columns ran: Peter Kenis, David Malley, Coco McPherson, Evan Schlansky, Jason Stutts, Sean Woods, and their fearless leader, Sarah Pratt. When you're on a quest for 100-percent accuracy, you want allies like these poring over every name and detail. (Of course, any errors in this book are entirely my own.)

Thanks to my literary agent, Joe Regal, who has that sparkly glow that surrounds people who are very good at their chosen professions, and to everyone at Regal Literary, especially Bess Reed and Lauren Schott.

I am proud to be published by Three Rivers Press, not least because of the excellent people who work there: my kick-ass editor, Carrie Thornton, of course, but also Brandi Bowles, Steve Ross, and Dan Rembert. I am also indebted to designer Kay Schuckhart, cover artist and illustrator Greg Kulick, publicist Jay Sones, and copy editor Joanna Kremer, all of whom did top-notch work.

Thanks to two people who made my job easier: Abby Royle, transcriber extraordinaire, and Eugene Schilder, my capable intern.

I am blessed by too many friends to thank them all individually. Many of them offered advice and encouragement while I was working on this book, and they are all dear to my heart. I am especially grateful to the New Year's Eve crew and the New York City Thursday-night Shadowfist clan. Let me also single out three friends by name: Deborah Suchman Zeolla, who rearranged her entire schedule to take my photograph; Bill Tipper, a gentleman, a scholar, and king of the wombats; and Rob Sheffield, who was always delighted to eat burritos with me and engage in long arguments about the Rock and Roll Hall of Fame.

Last but most certainly not least, I want to thank my wonderful wife, Jen, who gives me strength and grace that I didn't know I had, and who has made my world a bigger, better place, one filled with flying pigs and impromptu brass bands.

ENDNOTES

In fact, I don't know everything.

Put it this way: I'm knowledgeable enough that I qualified to be a contestant on *Jeopardy!* but when I was on the show (in the spring of 2000), I came in second place, winning a trip to France. (I still blame the buzzers, as does just about everyone who's ever lost on that show—once you're there, it turns out that everyone playing the game is smart, so victory comes down in large part to hand-eye coordination.)

So there's no shame in saying that I drew on other sources when answering the questions in this book. For some replies, I consulted as many as a dozen outside books and articles, making sure that I had my facts straight. If you're interested in further research on any of the topics in the book, this section should tell you where I drew upon other writers' work and let you delve deeper yourself. This isn't an exhaustive bibliography, for reasons of both space and sanity, but I've endeavored to provide the most useful and pertinent sources for each question. All URLs are, of course, valid at time of publication; if they no longer seem to work, I suggest the Internet Wayback Machine for cached versions of the pages.

I did get a Daily Double on *Jeopardy!*, by the way; they wanted to know in what category Burning Spear won a Grammy. I frantically riffled through all the possibilities, settling on "Best Album by Reggae Duo or Group"—and then realized I was completely overthinking matters. "What is reggae?" I said and received an approving nod from Alex Trebek. These endnotes are for my fellow overthinkers.

CHAPTER 1: **Mystery Achievement**

page 6 Does Stevie Wonder have a sense of smell?

"Stevie Wonder" by John Rockwell in *The Rolling Stone Illustrated History of Rock & Roll, Third Edition,* p. 293 (Random House, New York, 1992).

"Random Notes" in *Rolling Stone,* October 11, 1973 (issue 145), p. 24.

"Stevie Wonder: A Portrait of the Artist" by Gail Mitchell, *Billboard,* December 11, 2004, pp. 15–18.

7 The Beatles' MBEs

The Beatles Anthology, pp. 181–184 (Chronicle Books, San Francisco, 2000).

9 Dave Grohl chewing gum

"Dave Grohl" by Austin Scaggs, *Rolling Stone,* June 12, 2003 (issue 924), p. 65.

See also the *Melody Maker* "Coolest People in Rock" 2000 article and Ian Winwood interview with Dave Grohl for the *NME 2005 Festival Guide,* both available at www.fooarchive.com.

10 "Rock Around the Clock" B-side

Fred Bronson, *The Billboard Book of Number One Hits,* fifth edition, p. 1 (Billboard Books, New York, 2003).

The "Atomic Platters" Web site:

http://www.atomicplatters.com/more.php?id=41_0_1_0_M

11 The Green Fairy

Author's email correspondence with Baz Luhrmann, circa October 2002.

12 "Anarchy in the U.K."

John Lydon, *Rotten: No Irish, No Blacks, No Dogs,* p. 270 (Hodder and Stoughton, London, 1994).

13 Farnsworth Bentley

Author interview with Derek Watkins, circa February 2004.

15 Radiohead's "Just"

http://www.greenplastic.com/discography/videography/just/index.php

16 Tom Waits's tattoo

"What's He Building in There?: An Interview with Tom Waits," by Barney Hoskins, *Mojo,* April 1999.

Waits has told variations of the story in many other interviews, as compiled at http://www.keeslau.com/TomWaitsSupplement/Topography/napoleones.htm.

17 Bono's height

Author interviews with six anonymous sources, circa February 2006.

www.u2faqs.com

18 Joe Strummer's marathons

Marcus Gray, *Last Gang in Town: The Story and Myth of the Clash,* pp. 387, 411–413, 420, 437 (Henry Holt, New York, 1996).

David Quantick, *The Clash,* p. 35 (Thunder's Mouth Press, New York, 2000).

19 *Pinkerton* map

Author interview with Rivers Cuomo, circa December 1996.

21 John Mayer's synaesthesia

Author interview with John Mayer, circa May 2002.

22 "Strawberry Fields Forever"

Liner notes by Mark Lewisohn to The Beatles *Anthology 2* CD release (Apple/Capitol, 1996), p. 30.

22 "Paul Is Dead"

Andru J. Reeve, *Turn Me On, Dead Man: The Beatles and the "Paul-Is-Dead" Hoax* (AuthorHouse, Bloomington, Indiana, 2004).

http://www.beatles-discography.com/index.html?
http://www.beatles-discography.com/appendicies/
paul-is-dead-clues.html

"Paul McCartney," 1974 *Rolling Stone* interview by Paul Gambaccini, as included in *The Rolling Stone Interviews: Talking with the Legends of Rock 'n' Roll 1967–1980,* p. 304 (Rolling Stone Press, New York, 1981).

CHAPTER 2: **Get Ur Freak On**

page 26 Rod Stewart's stomach pumping

"Rod Stewart" by Rob Tannenbaum, *Details,* August 1995, p. 154.

27 Bee Gees' porno movie

Timothy White, *Rock Lives,* p. 488 (Henry Holt, New York, 1990).
Robin Gibb's comment notwithstanding, the correct title of the
movie appears to be *The Kinky Ladies of Bourbon Street.*

28 Mick Jagger/David Bowie

Angela Bowie, *Backstage Passes: Life on the Wild Side with
David Bowie,* pp. 240–241 (Putnam, New York, 1993).

Snopes Urban Legends Reference Page: http://www
.snopes.com/music/artists/bowie.htm.

Victor Bockris, *Keith Richards: The Biography,* pp. 200–204 (Da
Capo, New York, 2003).

30 The Arab Strap

Author interview with Malcolm Middleton, circa June 2003.

31 Elvis Presley's proclivities

Peter Whitmer, *The Inner Elvis,* pp. 192–193, 212 (Hyperion, New
York, 1996).

32 2 Live Crew

"The Crude Lyrics in 2 Live Crew's Rap" by Joel Selvin, *The San
Francisco Chronicle,* June 11, 1990, p. A18.

33 Bebe Buell and Elvis Costello

Bebe Buell with Victor Bockris, *Rebel Heart: An American Rock
'n' Roll Journey,* especially pp.185–203 and 231–259 (St. Martin's
Press, New York, 2001).

"Bebe Talk" by Bebe Buell, *Details,* July 1996, pp. 86–94.

Elvis Costello, liner notes to 2002 Rhino reissue of Elvis Costello
and the Attractions' *Armed Forces,* p. 12.

Author conversation with Bebe Buell, circa September 2003.

35 Best-endowed male stars

The "World Famous Penis Chart" at www.metalsludge.tv.

"Mark McGrath of Sugar Ray" by Chris Mundy, *Rolling Stone,* February 19, 1999 (issue 806), p. 27.

36 Marvin Gaye and porn

David Ritz, *Divided Soul: The Life of Marvin Gaye,* especially pp. 178–181, 258, 295–296, 325–334 (Omnibus Press, London, 1995).

37 The Raeletts

Ray Charles and David Ritz, *Brother Ray: Ray Charles' Own Story,* pp. 167–172 (Dial Press, New York, 1978).

Michael Lydon, *Ray Charles: Man and Music,* pp. 145–146, 319–320 (Payback Press, Edinburgh, 1999).

39 "Summer of '69"

"Outside the Wall: An Interview with Bryan Adams" by Alastair McLean, REG—The International Roger Waters Fan Club Newsletter/Magazine #18 (also http://www.rogerwaters.org/adamsint.html).

"Bryan Adams—writer, photographer—sings tonight" by Sarah D'Esti Miller, *Binghamton Press & Sun Bulletin,* April 4, 2001.

40 Joan Baez and John Lennon

"Joan Baez," 1983 *Rolling Stone* interview by Kurt Loder, as included in *The Rolling Stone Interviews: The 1980s,* pp. 89–90 (St. Martin's Press, New York, 1989).

CHAPTER 3: I Hold the Title

page 44 Maroon 5

Author interview with Adam Levine, circa October 2003.

44 *Atom Heart Mother*

Nicholas Schaffner, *Saucerful of Secrets: The Pink Floyd Odyssey,* p. 154 (Delta, New York, 1992).

45 "Le Freak"

Author interview with Nile Rodgers, circa May 2004.

46 *Kid A*

"Sound and Fury" by Andrew Smith, *The Observer* (UK), October 1, 2000.

"The Post-Rock Band" by Gerald Marzorati, *The New York Times Magazine,* October 1, 2000.

"I Can See the Monsters" by David Cavanagh, *Q,* October 2000.

47 "Norwegian Wood"

David Sheff, *The Playboy Interviews with John Lennon & Yoko Ono,* pp. 150–151 (New English Library, Kent, 1982).

Barry Miles, *Paul McCartney: Many Years from Now,* pp. 270–271 (Henry Holt, New York, 1997).

49 Double Rs

Author interview with Chingy, circa August 2003.

49 *"The Spaghetti Incident?"*

Author interviews with Duff McKagan and Slash, circa June 2004.

CHAPTER 4: Lawyers, Guns, and Money

page 54 CDs on Tuesdays

Author interview with Joe McFadden, circa August 2003.

55 Billy Ocean

Joel Whitburn, *The Billboard Book of Top 40 Hits,* eighth edition (Billboard Books, New York, 2004).

56 Import CDs

Author interview with John Voigtmann, circa January 2003.

57 Most covered song

The Guinness Book of World Records opts for "Yesterday"; see http://www.guinnessworldrecords.com/content_pages/record.asp?recordid=50867.

Joel Whitburn's Pop Memories 1890–1954: The History of American Popular Music (Hal Leonard, 1991).

58 James Brown fines

Author interviews with Bobby Byrd and James Brown, both circa April 2004.

59 Simultaneous number one and number two singles

Joel Whitburn, *The Billboard Book of Top 40 Hits,* eighth edition (Billboard Books, New York, 2004).

60 George Harrison songwriting deal

Barry Miles, *Paul McCartney: Many Years from Now,* pp. 146–147, 178–179 (Henry Holt, New York, 1997).

Bill Harry, *The Ultimate Beatles Encyclopedia,* p. 499 (Hyperion, New York, 1993).
www.beatles-discography.com, also compiled as Craig Cross, *The Beatles: Day-by-Day, Song-by-Song, Record-by-Record* (iUniverse, 2005).

Mark Lewisohn, *The Complete Beatles Recording Sessions: The Official Story of the Abbey Road Years 1962–1970* (Hamlyn, London, 2004).

61 CDs self-destructing

Author interview with Ted Sheldon, circa February 2003.

62 Breeders covers

BMI archives.

63 Number two singles

Christopher G. Feldman, *The Billboard Book of No. 2 Singles,* p. 280 (Billboard Books, New York, 2000).

64 Neil Young's *Comes a Time*

Scott Young, *Neil and Me* (McClelland & Stewart, Toronto, 1997).

CHAPTER 5: **I'm with the Band**

page 66 Plaster Casters

Author interview with Cynthia Plaster Caster, circa February 2003.

67 The Butter Queen

"Elton John: The Playboy Interview" by David Standish and Eugenie Ross-Leming, *Playboy*, January 1976, pp. 57–70.

David Cassidy with Chip Deffaa, *C'mon, Get Happy: Fear and Loathing on the Partridge Family Bus,* pp. 112–114 (Warner Books, New York, 1994).

Author interview with Barbara Cope, circa October 2002.

68 Sweet Connie

"Confessions of a Rock 'n' Roll Groupie" by Connie Hamzy with Melanie Wells, *Penthouse,* January 1992.

"Oldest Living Confederate Groupie Tells All" by Rodger Cambria, *Spin*, February 2005.

69 Led Zeppelin versus the shark

Richard Cole with Richard Trubo, *Stairway to Heaven: Led Zeppelin Uncensored*, pp. 88–93 (HarperCollins, New York, 2002).

Charles R. Cross and Erik Flannigan, *Led Zeppelin: Heaven and Hell*, p. 170 (Harmony Books, New York, 1991).

"Cash for Questions: Robert Plant," *Q*, August 2002.

Author interview with Carmine Appice, circa June 2004.

CHAPTER 6: **I'm in the Band**

page 74 Chevy Chase and Steely Dan

"The Return of Steely Dan" by Andy Gill, *Mojo,* October 1995.

www.steelydan.com (FAQ and BBC Chat, March 4, 2000).

75 Sex Pistols' original vocalist

Lee Wood, *The Sex Pistols Diary: Sex Pistols Day by Day,* p. 3 (Omnibus Press, London, 1988).

John Lydon, *Rotten: No Irish, No Blacks, No Dogs,* pp. 81–82 (Hodder and Stoughton, London, 1994).

76 Longest-running bands

It should be noted that the answer covers only bands of major stature; that is, your dad and his three best friends may have played every Friday night at the local pub for the past fifty years, and yet they don't qualify. The answer has other gray areas, mostly centering around the fact that taking a few years off between albums is standard operating procedure as bands enter their second decade, but surprisingly difficult to distinguish from a group that has stealthily broken up and then gotten back together; Hall & Oates, for example, have arguably logged thirty-seven years together, but were on "hiatus" and released no albums between 1990 and 1997. For more information on the Osmonds, check out "An American Family" by Chris Heath in the July 1995 issue of *Details.*

77 Eminem/D12

Anthony Bozza, *Whatever You Say I Am: The Life and Times of Eminem* (Crown, New York, 2003).

Nick Hasted, *The Dark Story of Eminem* (Omnibus Press, London, 2003).

78 Mick Jones fired from the Clash

Marcus Gray, *Last Gang in Town: The Story and Myth of the Clash,* pp. 422–423 (Henry Holt, New York, 1996).

79 Bez

Author reporting and interviews with Shaun Ryder and Bez, circa October 1995.

CHAPTER 7: **Blood on Blood**

page 84 Steven Tyler and Liv Tyler

Author interview with Steven Tyler, circa August 1999.

85 Brian Eno

"50 Eno Moments" by Tim de Lisle, *The Independent on Sunday* (UK), May 10, 1998.

85 Hank Williams Jr./ Kid Rock

http://www.vh1.com/artists/news/1451542/12182001/ williams_jr_hank.jhtml

86 Kurt Cobain and *Live Through This*

Author interview with Kurt Cobain, circa August 1993.

"Blonde on Blonde" by Courtney Love and Stevie Nicks, *Spin,* October 1997.

"Whose Song Is It Anyway?" by Kathleen Wilson, *The Stranger,* 1998.
http://livenirvana.com/sessions/index.html: click through to October 1993.

Poppy Z. Brite, *Courtney Love: The Real Story* (Simon & Schuster, New York, 1997).

"Love Says Corgan Hasn't Turned Her into a Pumpkin" by Karen Thomas, *USA Today,* June 19, 1998, p. 5E.

"The Innovators: Courtney Love" by Phoebe Reilly on *Spin*'s Web site: http://www.spinmagazine.com/spin20extra/2005/09/ spin20_courtney/.

90 "You Ain't Seen Nothin' Yet"

Author interview with Randy Bachman, circa June 2003.

Fred Bronson, *The Billboard Book of Number One Hits,* fifth
edition, p. 382 (Billboard Books, New York, 2003).

91 The White Stripes

The Glorious Noise Web site has copies of both their marriage
license (http://www.gloriousnoise.com/?pg=white_stripes_
married.php) and their divorce certificate (http://www
.gloriousnoise.com/?pg=white_stripes_divorced.php).

92 ABBA and the Nazis

Carl Magnus Palm, *Bright Lights, Dark Shadows: The Real Story
of Abba,* pp. 42–45, 360–364 (Omnibus Press, London, 2002).

92 Twins

The Rolling Stone Encyclopedia of Rock & Roll, third edition
(Fireside Press, New York, 2001).

93 Jim Gordon

"When the Voices Took Over" by Barry Rehfeld, *Rolling Stone,*
June 6, 1985 (issue 449), pp. 17–22.

94 Victoria and Lucinda Williams

Author interview with Victoria Williams, circa September 2002.

95 Dustin and Mike Diamond

"Dustin Diamond" by Josh Modell, *The Onion,* January 30, 2002
(also at the Onion AV Club online archives: http://www
.avclub.com/content/node/22692).

96 The Mansons and the Wilsons

Jon Stebbins, *Dennis Wilson: The Real Beach Boy,* pp. 129–141
(ECW Press, Toronto, 2000).

97 Gibby and Mr. Peppermint

Author interview with Gibby Haynes, circa July 2004. Let it be
noted that the interview took place at New York City's late,
lamented Second Avenue Deli over pastrami sandwiches.

"Jerry Haynes" by Marty Primeau, *Dallas Morning News,*
July 12, 1987.

"A Strange Twist for Mr. Peppermint" by Maryln Schwartz, *Dallas Morning News*, May 23, 1989.

CHAPTER 8: **Dirty Deeds Done Dirt Cheap**

page 102 Ohio Players killing a girl during "Love Rollercoaster"
Author interview with Jimmy "Diamond" Williams, circa July 2002.

103 Steely Dan versus the Eagles
"Conversations with Don Henley and Glenn Frey," liner notes by Cameron Crowe to the Eagles' *The Very Best Of* CD release (Warner Music Group, 2003), pp. 21–22.

104 Chuck Berry's bathroom cameras
"Chuck Berry Taped Women, Suit Charges" by Ralph Dummit, *St. Louis Post-Dispatch,* December 27, 1989, p. 4A.

"Women Sue Berry, Charge He Took Bathroom Videos" by Marianna Riley, *St. Louis Post-Dispatch,* June 30, 1990, p. 3A.

"Berry Lawsuit Settled; Rock Legend Denies Videotaping Women" by Al Stamborski, *St. Louis Post-Dispatch,* November 1, 1994, p. 1A.

105 Son of Sam
Author interview with Daryl Hall, circa March 2003.

106 The Kinks in the USA
Jon Savage, *The Kinks: The Official Autobiography,* pp. 46–52 (Faber and Faber, London, 1984).

Ray Davies, *X-Ray: The Unauthorized Autobiography,* pp. 238–260 (Penguin, London, 1995).

108 Led Zeppelin versus George Harrison
Charles R. Cross and Erik Flannigan, *Led Zeppelin: Heaven and Hell,* p. 133 (Harmony Books, New York, 1991).

109 Jim Morrison whipping it out

Ray Manzarek, *Light My Fire: My Life with the Doors,*
pp. 310–323 (G. P. Putnam's Sons, New York, 1998).

110 Smashing Pumpkins versus Pavement

"In the News" by Neil Strauss, *Rolling Stone,* May 5, 1995 (issue
681), p. 15.

"Smashing Pumpkins" by David Fricke, *Rolling Stone,* November 16, 1995 (issue 721).

"Underfoot: Pavement Pounds the Pumpkins" by Jess Barron,
originally wildweb.com in November 1999, now archived at
http://www.poprocks.com/articles/pavement.html.

111 Frank Zappa and pornography

Neil Slaven, *Electric Don Quixote: The Definitive Story of Frank
Zappa,* pp. 40–44 (Omnibus Press, London, 2003).

112 Gregg Allman's foot-shootin' party

Author interview with Gregg Allman, circa August 1999.

Scott Freeman, *Midnight Riders: The Story of the Allman
Brothers Band* (Little, Brown, Boston, 1995).

CHAPTER 9: **Close Encounters of the Rock Kind**

page 116 Axl Rose and Depeche Mode

Dave Thompson, *Depeche Mode: Some Great Reward,*
pp. 207–208 (St. Martin's Press, New York, 1994).

117 Peter Wolf and David Lynch

Author interview with Peter Wolf, circa August 2003.

118 Sheryl Crow and Eric Clapton

Richard Buskin, *Sheryl Crow: No Fool to This Game,* p. 189
(Billboard Books, New York, 2002).

119 Eminem and Dr. Dre

Anthony Bozza, *Whatever You Say I Am: The Life and Times of Eminem* (Crown, New York, 2003).

Nick Hasted, *The Dark Story of Eminem* (Omnibus Press, London, 2003).

120 Don Henley and Stevie Nicks

"Blonde on Blonde" by Courtney Love and Stevie Nicks, *Spin*, October 1997.

"Too Many Choices" by Christopher Connelly, *GQ*, August 1991, p. 143.

121 Prince and Bob Marley

Per Nilsen, *DanceMusicSexRomance: Prince—The First Decade*, pp. 61–62 (Firefly, London, 1999).

122 Nico and Jim Morrison

Ray Manzarek, *Light My Fire: My Life with the Doors*, pp. 218–221 (G. P. Putnam's Sons, New York, 1998).

Nico Icon (film directed by Susanne Ofteringer, 1995).

Victor Bockris, *Transformer: The Lou Reed Story*, p. 107 (Da Capo, New York, 1997).

Legs McNeil and Gillian McCain, *Please Kill Me: The Uncensored Oral History of Punk* (Penguin, New York, 1996).

Joe Ambrose, *Gimme Danger: The Story of Iggy Pop*, pp. 67–71 (Omnibus Press, London, 2002).

123 The Darkness and Neil Diamond

Author interview with Justin Hawkins, circa March 2004.

CHAPTER 10: **I Write the Songs**

page 126 Elton John's "Tiny Dancer"

Author interview with Bernie Taupin, circa August 2002.

128 Led Zeppelin and Tolkien

John Paul Jones online interview with America OnLine members, December 17, 1997.

129 Van Halen's "Everybody Wants Some!!"

David Lee Roth, *Crazy from the Heat,* pp. 115–116 (Hyperion, New York, 1997).

129 Interpol's "PDA"

Author interview with Paul Banks, circa July 2003.

130 United States of Springsteen

Author research.

131 Missy Elliott's "Gossip Folks"

Author research.

132 Crosby, Stills & Nash's "Our House"

Author interviews with David Crosby and Graham Nash (but not Stephen Stills), circa April 2004.

A. M. Nolan, *Rock 'n' Roll Road Trip: The Ultimate Guide to the Sites, the Shrines, and the Legends Across America,* p. 207 (Pharos, New York, 1992).

134 Donna Summer's "Bad Girls"

Author interview with Donna Summer, circa May 2004.

135 Fountains of Wayne's "Hackensack"

Mark Binelli interview with Adam Schlesinger, circa October 2003 (thanks, Mark).

136 The Allman Brothers' "Elizabeth Reed"

Scott Freeman, *Midnight Riders: The Story of the Allman Brothers Band,* pp. 73–74 (Little, Brown, Boston, 1995).

Author interview with Dickey Betts, circa July 1999.

137 Title of the song appears only as last line

Author research (with help from Christian Ruzich and Robert Rossney). Excluded are songs in which the only lyrics of the song are the title, uttered once.

137 The White Stripes' "Hotel Yorba"

Denise Sullivan, *The White Stripes: Sweethearts of the Blues,* p. 4 (Backbeat Books, San Francisco, 2004).

138 Rickie Lee Jones, "Chuck E.'s in Love"

Timothy White, *Rock Lives*, p. 683 (Henry Holt, New York, 1990).

139 Paul Simon's "Me and Julio Down by the Schoolyard"

"Paul Simon," 1972 *Rolling Stone* interview by Jon Landau, as included in *The Rolling Stone Interviews: Talking with the Legends of Rock 'n' Roll 1967–1980*, p. 214 (Rolling Stone Press, New York, 1981).

140 Wilco's *Yankee Hotel Foxtrot*

Greg Kot, *Wilco: Learning How to Die*, pp. 221–226 (Broadway Books, New York, 2004).

141 Barry Manilow's songwriting

Author research.

142 Audioslave's "Cochise"

Author interview with Tom Morello, circa November 2002.

143 Elton John's "Someone Saved My Life Tonight"

Author research, including conversations with British relatives (thanks, Mom).

143 Randy Newman urban songs

Author research.

144 "Angels had guitars before they even had wings"

Meat Loaf, *Bat Out of Hell II: Back into Hell* (MCA CD release, 1993).

Jim Steinman, *Bad for Good* (CD reissue of 1981 Epic Release).

Joel Whitburn, *The Billboard Book of Top 40 Hits,* eighth edition (Billboard Books, New York, 2004).

145 Carly Simon's "You're So Vain"

Simon has collected many of the articles written about the song on her Web site, www.carlysimon.com.

" 'So Vain' Mystery Answers," *Downtown Express* (New York), December 16–22, 2005, p. 2.

Robert Christgau, *Rock Albums of the '70s: A Critical Guide,* p. 353 (Da Capo, New York, 1990).

CHAPTER 11: Sex, Drugs, and Rock 'n' Roll

page 150 Jimi Hendrix and LSD

David Henderson, *'Scuse Me While I Kiss the Sky: The Life of Jimi Hendrix,* p. 349 (Omnibus, London, 2002).

Author interview with Jim Fricke, circa February 2004.

152 Coldplay and cocaine

Martin Roach, *Coldplay: Nobody Said It Was Easy,* pp. 38–40 (Omnibus, London, 2003).

152 Rolling Stones bust at Redlands

"As Tears Go By" by Scott Cohen, *Spin,* August 1987, pp. 54–55.

Christopher Sandford, *Mick Jagger: Primitive Cool,* pp. 99–118 (St. Martin's Press, New York, 1993).

154 Grateful Dead and diet pills

David Shenk and Steve Silberman, *Skeleton Key: A Dictionary for Deadheads,* pp. 230–231 (Main Street, New York, 1994).

154 The Beatles and LSD

The Beatles Anthology, pp. 177–179 (Chronicle Books, San Francisco, 2000).

156 *The Wizard of Oz* versus *Dark Side of the Moon*

Author research, aided by NyQuil.

"Dark Side of 'The Matrix' " by Rob Sheffield, *Rolling Stone,* May 15, 2003 (issue 922), p. 46.

CHAPTER 12: **Studio System**

page 162 "Gunter gleben glousen globen"

Author interview with Joe Elliott, circa December 2003.

163 Donna Summer's "Love to Love You Baby"

Author interview with Donna Summer, circa May 2004.

"Gaudy Reign of the Disco Queen" by Jay Cocks, *Time,* December 4, 1978.

164 Prince and Madonna

Paul Zollo, *Songwriters on Songwriting: Expanded Fourth Edition,* pp. 618–619 (Da Capo, New York, 2003).

165 Pink Floyd's *Household Objects*

Nick Mason, *Inside Out: A Personal History of Pink Floyd,* pp. 194, 208 (Chronicle Books, San Francisco, 2005).

Nicholas Schaffner, *Saucerful of Secrets: The Pink Floyd Odyssey,* p. 187 (Delta, New York, 1992).

167 Chic's "Good Times"

Author interview with Nile Rodgers, circa May 2004.

169 The Beatles' "Yellow Submarine"

Bill Harry, *The Ultimate Beatles Encyclopedia,* pp. 712–713 (Hyperion, New York, 1993).

The Pythons, *The Pythons: Autobiography,* pp. 234–235 (Thomas Dunne Books, New York, 2003).

170 Phil Spector and "Be My Baby"

Author's email correspondence with Phil Spector, April 2004.

CHAPTER 13: **Say My Name, Say My Name**

page 176 Iggy Pop

Legs McNeil and Gillian McCain, *Please Kill Me: The Uncensored Oral History of Punk* (Penguin, New York, 1996).

Joe Ambrose, *Gimme Danger: The Story of Iggy Pop,* pp. 6, 42–43 (Omnibus Press, London, 2002).

177 Jimmy Eat World

Author interview with Zach Lind, circa October 2002.

178 The E Street Band

"David Sancious Serenade" by Bill Flanagan, *Musician*, July 1991.

And http://www.beyondthepalace.com/newjersey/ estreet1.html has a photo of the intersection of E Street and Tenth Avenue.

179 t.A.T.u.

http://www.mtv.com/news/yhif/tatu/

180 DMX

E.A.R.L.: The Autobiography of DMX, as told to Smokey D. Fontaine, pp. 76–77 (HarperCollins, New York, 2003).

180 Pearl Jam

Kim Neely, *Five Against One: The Pearl Jam Story,* pp. 74–76 (Penguin, New York, 1998).

181 R.E.M.

Marcus Gray, *It Crawled From the South: An R.E.M. Companion,* pp. 194–215 (Da Capo, New York, 1997).

182 Weezer

John D. Luerssen, *Rivers' Edge: The Weezer Story,* pp. 63–64 (ECW Press, Toronto, 2004).

183 Foo Fighters

Ron Goulart, editor, *The Encyclopedia of American Comics: From 1897 to the Present,* p. 340 (Facts on File, New York, 1990).

"Dave Grohl" by Eric Brace, *UNo Mas* magazine (http:// www.unomas.com/features/foofighters.html).

184 Velvet Revolver

Author interview with Duff McKagan, circa June 2004.

185 Circle Jerks and Gun Club

"Preachin' the Blues" by Jay Hinman (http://www.furious.com/perfect/gunclub.html).

"Ex-Gun Club Leader Dead" by Fred "Phast Phreddie" Patterson, *Addicted to Noise,* April 2, 1996 (http://pages .sbcglobal.net/dante/last/jlp.html).

186 Jay-Z / Hova

"Get Carter" by Ted Kessler, *The Guardian* (UK), January 25, 2003.

CHAPTER 14: Long Black Veil

page 188 James Taylor's "Fire and Rain"

Timothy White, *Long Ago and Far Away: James Taylor—His Life and Music,* pp. 141–143 (Omnibus, London, 2002).

189 Jeff Porcaro

Author interview with anonymous source, circa September 2003.

190 Philip "Taylor" Kramer

"Far Out" by Richard Leiby, *Washington Post,* October 6, 1996, p. F1.

"The Vanishing," *Maxim,* October 1999.

191 David Ruffin

Nick Talevski, *The Encyclopedia of Rock Obituaries,* pp. 369–370 (Omnibus, London, 1999).

192 Onstage deaths

Nick Talevski, *The Encyclopedia of Rock Obituaries* (Omnibus, London, 1999).

192 Keith Relf

Keith Shadwick, *Led Zeppelin: 1968–1980,* p. 255 (Backbeat, San Francisco, 2005).

www.obituariestoday.com

International Relf Society Web site: http://members.madasafish.com/~relf/rock.html

"Live Fast . . . The Stars Who Died Young," *The Independent* (UK), October 17, 2002, contains the erroneous bathtub story.

193 Donny Hathaway

"Lalah Hathaway Grateful for Her Father's Gifts" by Shelah Moody, *San Francisco Chronicle,* October 20, 2005, p. E2.

Nick Talevski, *The Encyclopedia of Rock Obituaries,* pp. 176 (Omnibus, London, 1999).

194 Johnny Ace

James M. Salem, *The Late Great Johnny Ace: And the Transition from R&B to Rock 'n' Roll,* pp. 69–70, 128–140 (University of Illinois Press, Urbana, 2001).

195 Keith Moon and Mama Cass

"One Last Touch of Nilsson" by Dawn Eden, *Goldmine,* April 29, 1994 (also archived at www.harrynilsson.com).

Dave Marsh, *Before I Get Old: The Story of the Who,* pp. 506–507 (St. Martin's Press, New York, 1983).

Nick Talevski, *The Encyclopedia of Rock Obituaries,* pp. 114, 294 (Omnibus, London, 1999).

"You Ask the Questions: Pete Townshend," *The Independent* (UK), February 13, 2002.

CHAPTER 15: **Do You Want to Know a Secret?**

page 199 Robert Johnson's soul

Barry Lee Pearson and Bill McCulloch, *Robert Johnson: Lost and Found*, pp. 65–69 (University of Illinois Press, Urbana, 2003).

Peter Guralnick, *Searching for Robert Johnson* (Plume, New York, 1998).

Elijah Wald, *Escaping the Delta: Robert Johnson and the Invention of the Blues* (Amistad, HarperCollins, 2004).

201 Ringo Starr's abilities

Paul Zollo, *Songwriters on Songwriting: Expanded Fourth Edition*, p. 717 (Da Capo, New York, 2003), contains the Lenny Kravitz quote.

David Sheff, *The Playboy Interviews with John Lennon & Yoko Ono*, p. 141 (New English Library, Kent, 1982).

203 Mick Jagger's grades

Christopher Sandford, *Mick Jagger: Primitive Cool*, pp. 37, 48 (St. Martin's Press, New York, 1994).

"Jagger Remembers: The Rolling Stone Interview" by Jann S. Wenner, *Rolling Stone*, December 14, 1995 (issue 723).

204 Kid Rock's escort service

"The Low Times and High Life of Kid Rock" by Chris Heath, *Rolling Stone*, June 22, 2000 (issue 843).

205 Billie Joe's projectile

Fred Bronson, *The Billboard Book of Number One Hits*, fifth edition, p. 229 (Billboard Books, New York, 2003).

206 Pete Townshend's windmill

"Pete Townshend: The Playboy Interview" by David Sheff, *Playboy,* February 1994.

207 Dr. Hook's cover

Conversation with Rik Elswit on The Well, www.well.com.

208 Bob Dylan's accident

Howard Sounes, *Down the Highway: The Life of Bob Dylan,* pp. 216–220 (Grove, New York, 2001).

"Scarred Bob Dylan Is Comin' Back" by Michael Iachetta, originally in the *New York Daily News,* May 1967, reprinted in *Bob Dylan: The Early Years—A Retrospective,* pp. 197–202 (Da Capo, New York, 1990).

Robert Shelton, *No Direction Home: The Life and Music of Bob Dylan,* pp. 374–378 (Da Capo, New York, 2003).

Bob Dylan, *Chronicles: Volume One,* pp. 114–115 (Simon & Schuster, New York, 2004).

211 Led Zeppelin's glyphs

Charles R. Cross and Erik Flannigan, *Led Zeppelin: Heaven and Hell,* pp. 122–126 (Harmony Books, New York, 1991).

"What do those four symbols on Led Zeppelin's fourth album mean?" Straight Dope staff report (http://www.straightdope.com/mailbag/mledzeppelin.html).

About the Author

In the name of journalism, Gavin Edwards has hiked the Great Wall of China, entered a demolition derby, and flown to Spain to participate in a food fight. He is a contributing editor at *Rolling Stone;* he has also written extensively on music, movies, and other topics for *Details, Spin, New York,* and *GQ,* among other publications. He is the author of the bestselling book *'Scuse Me While I Kiss This Guy and Other Misheard Lyrics,* as well as its multiple sequels, page-a-day calendars, and temporary tattoos. In his capacity as one of the nation's leading rock-lyrics experts, he has appeared on the *Today* show, MTV, and hundreds of radio programs. In his capacity as a freelance know-it-all, he has appeared as a contestant on *Jeopardy!* (where he won a trip to France). He lives in New York City with his wife, Jen, and their son, Strummer.